# Tales of the Unexplained

## Steph Young

**Copyright 2019 Steph Young**

**All Rights Reserved**

# Introduction

Join Join me for some true tales of mystery, of the most cryptic kind. In this book there are some extremely strange and baffling true stories of unexplained mysteries, and the cast of characters who star in them. Stories of unexplained mysteries that yearn to be solved.

Why was a man found in the same spot he disappeared in, but 4 years later, with a hole in his head that no surgeons could explain, and what did this have to do with a séance, doppelgangers, and the assassination of Abraham Lincoln?

How did an introverted lady die on the top of an ancient fairy mound, on a remote island: her face locked in an expression of terror?

What happened to Elisa Lam, found dead in a water tower on the top of a hotel roof. Who were the two men who came to see her, and what was in the mystery box they gave her? Why did the location of her grave stone match the zip code of the last place she was seen? plus many more mysterious cases...

All of these strange and curious stories I have written about over the last six years, across a number of my previous books. They continue to intrigue me, and while some of my readers may be familiar with some of these cryptic tales, I present them once more, in much deeper format, delving more deeply into these mysterious events and the characters who feature in them.... Mysteries which still have yet to be solved.

These stories are some of the most intriguing, enigmatic, and ultimately unfathomable true tales I have ever come across and they continue to fascinate and completely puzzle me. Some of these tales can also be heard on my podcast on iTunes: Tales of Mystery Unexplained.

Who doesn't love an unexplained, cryptic, and beguiling mystery?

# Table of Contents

Introduction .......................................................................... 2

Chapter One: "I'm looking for the Beast" .......................... 5

Chapter Two: The Mystery Box ......................................... 10

Chapter Three: The strange disappearnce of Donald ...... 73

Chapter Four: I'm a freak ................................................. 96

Chapter Five: Taken by the Fey ....................................... 112

Chapter Six: The Ghost Boys ........................................... 149

Chapter Seven: Missing: Returned Dead of Fright ......... 153

Chapter Eight: The Hairy Hands ..................................... 158

Chapter Nine: Folie a dieux ............................................ 162

Chapter Ten: Hecate in the ancient Woods ................... 179

Chapter Eleven: The Island Mystery .............................. 182

Chapter Twelve: American Dyatlov ................................ 206

## Chapter One:

## "I'm looking for the Beast"

According to the Prescott Courier of Arizona, in 1988 on the night of Halloween, a man called Larry Rivers was driving along a dirt road in the desert when he came across a man out walking alone. Mr Rivers slowed his car down and after opening his window, he asked the man; "What are you doing out here?"

"I'm looking for the beast," came the reply from the man on foot.

The man's name was David Stone, and he was wearing just a T-shirt and shorts, despite it being winter. This would later be believed to be the last time he was seen alive. Nearly a week later, he was officially reported missing, although he would not actually be found until four years later. Former Deputy Sheriff, William Cavliere said, "It's just about the strangest thing that ever happened round here."

When David Stone was reported missing, the search effort to find him was massive. Planes flew over-head, teams of searchers covered and re-covered the ground with bloodhounds. His tracks were found; but it seemed they simply just stopped, in the middle of no-where. There was no sign of him. His footprints just suddenly stopped.

The missing man, David Stone, had been travelling en-route from San Diego to El Paso in Texas, where he was due to be best-man at a friend's wedding. When he didn't arrive for the wedding, his father contacted all of the Sheriff's offices between San Diego and El Paso. None of them had received any reports about him, but the Sheriffs in New Mexico did subsequently locate his car abandoned on route 80, approximately fifteen miles south of Forks Road, parked at an odd angle.

The search for him lasted almost two weeks until it was called off. It would not be until four years later that three hunters stumbled across some bones in a granite outcrop in the desert, about a mile from the highway. Ken Melhberg, one of the hunters, said that he thought at first they were animal bones, but as he got closer to them, the first bone he picked up looked to him like a human jaw-bone. He realized then that the bones were probably not animal at all; they looked distinctly human. The hunter said the skull appeared to be shattered from the back, but the exact cause of the missing man's death was unable to be determined by the medical examiner, Dr Mani Ehteshami. He said, "He did not sustain any injury before or at the time of his death." Although his skull was in pieces, the Dr. believed this was due to animal predation.

No personal items were found with the bones; no car keys, wallet, clothes. They were all missing. The only thing that was found, were the remains of his shoes. Leader of the County Search team, Ralph Dawdy said that their search for the missing man was; "One of the strangest" in his long years of co-ordinated searches. The reason for this is that when David Stone walked into the desert, he left behind him some very mysterious and hard to fathom clues. He left his car near some pyramid shaped mountains, and as searchers followed his initial trail, which led them northwest from his car, they came across a pile of small rocks that appeared to have been formed into a pyramid shape and enclosed by a triangle of rocks.

The following day, the searchers found another pyramid of rocks further on, and beside this lay the missing man's Rolex watch. Mr Stone had been a very successful Stockbroker and he was wealthy enough to have been able to afford a Rolex. A couple of miles further on, the searchers discovered some writing in the sand of the desert. As they looked more closely at the writing, they realized that it was the Fibonacci sequence of numbers, which is 0.1.1.2.3.5.8.13.21, except in this case, instead of the traditional ending of the number 21, it ended at 18. Why would David Stone change the configuration of the sequence? Over the years, people have theorized that this subtle alteration may have been Stone's way of signalling that he needed help; that he was leaving a sign that he was in trouble and needed help. But, if he did need help, what was happening to him?

The bloodhounds led the searchers on a 13-mile trek, following Stone's scent close to Highway 80, where it then just stopped. In his abandoned car, investigators discovered a note which said; "They think the WORD is in the safe. Six knives in Rob's room. You buy your tea and you takes your chances Halloween...."

What did this message mean? And what did it have to do with Stone's disappearance? Why was he building pyramids in the sand and writing the Fibonacci sequence deliberately wrongly? And even more strangely, what did he mean when he told the driver who stopped to ask if he was alright, "I'm looking for the beast....?"

## Chapter Two:

## The Mystery Box

What was in the mystery box? And did this have anything to do with the synchronicity of the two Zip codes….? The new revelations about Elisa Lam.

For anyone has read some of my earlier books, they may recall that in "Something in the Woods" in 2014, I discuss the strange case of Elisa Lam, which was very current at the time. I have spent a considerable amount of time over the last few months revisiting this case. The fate of Elisa Lam is a tale of tragedy, synchronicity, and perhaps of how the hunter became the prey in a game that was quite possibly crafted, as Gnostics would say, aeons ago and put into play by shadowy figures of dark power, across centuries. Elisa Lam's unexplained death is a deeply mysterious story, full of unanswered questions which yearn for revelation of the method, and yet the path to truth lies shrouded in obscurity, layered in riddles, and revolving in astonishing synchronicities.

The baffling unsolved death of Elisa Lam seemed to grip much of the world in February 2013, largely due to the bizarre video of her in an elevator just before she vanished. She was gone for 19 days. The video capturing her last known movements was taken from what was strangely said to have been the only security camera in the Cecil Hotel in downtown Los Angeles. LAPD released the footage of her inside the elevator, in an appeal for information about her whereabouts after her parents reported that they had not heard from her, and that this was highly unusual. An official missing person's case was opened, and the world became transfixed by Elisa inside the elevator.

Her behaviour was very odd, playful perhaps in moments, but the overall tone was incredibly eerie and sinister. It was as though she was in a desperate fight for life. Her enemy however, was both unknown and unseen.

It would not be until guests staying at the hotel began to report to staff, 2 weeks later, that the water in their rooms tasted most odd, that she would be found; naked, dead, and floating in one of the water towers on the roof of the hotel. In June 2013, authorities determined that Elisa Lam's death was 'accidental,' and caused by her own hand. Many crucial questions however have been left unanswered. One of which is; why would she climb over 15 feet up the side of a water-tower, on a roof at night, without her glasses, alone, and climb in? Another question, is what is happening to her in the very disturbing footage inside the elevator on the night she disappeared? Captured in immemorial now, it is chilling and unnerving to watch her. There is something very wrong here. She is seen entering the hotel elevator, pressing lots of buttons quickly, and then peeking out of the open elevator door into the corridor several times, while she waits for the elevator to close.

Its almost as though she is fearful that someone is after her, and perhaps they were. Peering along the hotel corridor, she waits as the door fails to close. Becoming increasingly agitated and distressed, we watch her begin to make increasingly odd gestures with her hands, then step out of the elevator, and she seems to hide in the corridor, but then quickly she returns, appearing terrified yet not fleeing the scene. Is her imagination playing tricks with her? Or is her killer there? Out of sight of the camera but lurking within inches of her? Strange shadows and movement can be seen inside the elevator, even face-type forms appear on the walls of the elevator. It looks like a scene from a horror movie. The video quality is not good however, and perhaps this accounts for the shadows and blurs and unnerving atmosphere, although in hindsight, we are watching it in the full knowledge that soon Elisa would die.

Some people think, that on studying the video, they catch sight of a foot in the corridor. Adding to the mystery is that for some reason, when the police released the footage of Elisa in the elevator, it had been chopped and cut, and the speed at which it plays had also been altered. It is missing one minute of viewing. The video appears to have no timestamp and nearly 1 minute has been cut from the footage. Why was some of the video cut out? What did it show? We are left to guess, given that the total footage is not available. The video is running slower than real-time, making her movements appear even more unhinged and inexplicable. At one point, she puts her hands out in front of her, as though feeling for something that is with her in the small enclosed space but is not visible. As we watch her, when she realizes there is an intangible invisible 'thing' enclosed with her, the expression of horror on her face grows and she wrenches her hands together in anguish, trying to stem the panic, bending her knees as the weakness of fear envelopes her; trying to maintain her grip on her sanity. Something she does not understand is happening to her. Her behaviour is of disorientation, shock, fear and perhaps hopelessness.

Some of the headlines after Elisa's death included, 'WATCH: CCTV footage shows woman 'stalked by ghost' shortly before death,' and, 'Real ghost caught on tape!' Did Elisa see a ghost? asks reporter John Kays for Newsblaze. 'Since it's captured on video, I do believe she did.' Why does the security tape look like she's talking to someone who is not visible, reaching her hands out and grasping the empty space? What is it that is making her so distressed and confused? She becomes terrified, wrenching her hands together, sinking into a crouch as she goes weak at the knees. She does not understand what is happening to her.

Some will say she was on drugs but none were found in her system. Whichever the answer, her tragic case has fascinated many.

Where are her glasses? She needed her glasses. Is this why she is fumbling in the elevator? She was on medication for bi-polar disorder. Had she forgotten to take her tablets? Or, was she having some kind of nervous breakdown? Isn't there simply a logical answer for her unorthodox behaviour and unexpected demise, without looking for riddles and enigma in her last known images?

Her behaviour is perhaps that of someone who has drugs in their system, and yet we will later learn that she had no illegal drugs in her body. At moments during this footage, perhaps we could interpret her behaviour as playful, coy, and flirtatious even, as she peeks out of the elevator. Perhaps she is playing hide and seek, or peek-a-boo with a person, a date perhaps, who is in the corridor. She is playing a game; childlike, innocent in her happiness, intimate in her emotions, isn't she? And yet, she ended up dead, re-birthed in water; her spirit released from her mortal body in what could even have been the most horrifying ritual; one that began, if not long before, when two mystery men walked into the hotel lobby and handed her a little box. This box has never been found, and what was inside of it has never been discovered, nor has the identity of the two men or why she would be meeting with them. A delivery man perhaps would be understandable; but it doesn't seem that's what these two men were. And, two delivery men? - The real purpose of their visit to Elisa at the Cecil Hotel, we may never know.

"We did see her come in with two gentlemen. They had a box, gave it to her," said LAPD Robbery and Homicide Detective Tennelle, who was investigating her unexplained disappearance and death. "She went up into - to the elevator. We never saw them again on video." What was in this mystery box? Yet before we go too far down a winding and dark path of riddles, conspiracy, coincidences and hidden meanings, perhaps we should begin at the beginning.

Canadian Elisa Lam was 21 years old when she disappeared in downtown Los Angeles. She'd taken some time off her University studies to travel alone. She had first travelled to San Diego, where she visited the City Zoo, and a 'Speakeasy,' where she lost her phone which had been borrowed from a friend. On January 26th, she arrived in L.A. after travelling alone by Amtrak. It's believed she had come to L.A., in part, to go to some of the places where scenes of her favourite movie, the atmospheric but sombre 'Drive' starring Ryan Gosling, had been filmed. During her trip, she phoned her parents on a daily basis. They were Hong Kong émigré's who owned a Vancouver restaurant. When she stopped phoning her parents, on January 31st, they called the LAPD, and an investigation to find her began. Elisa had planned to stay 4 nights at the Cecil Hotel and then move on to the next stop on what she had called her 'West Coast tour.' During her time in L.A. she had explored downtown, including visiting a book store.

On the afternoon of January 31st, her last known day alive, she had visited 'The Last Bookstore,' located just a few blocks from the Hotel. There, she had purchased some books and records to take back to Canada with her, as presents for family and friends. Katie Orphan, the Bookstore's manager remembers her as, "Very outgoing, very lively, very friendly, talking about what book she was getting and whether or not what she was getting would be too heavy for her to carry around as she travelled."

Six days later, on February 6th, LAPD's Robbery and Homicide Division held a press conference appealing for help from the public to find a young Canadian tourist who had disappeared. The police described her disappearance as "suspicious." Six days after this, the police released the bizarre video footage of Elisa in the hotel elevator.

5 days after the release of the erratic movements of Elisa in the elevator, hotel guests began to complain that the water coming from their taps tasted strange and had a dark colouring. Annette Suzuki was among the guests staying at the hotel when she, among several other residents, noticed that the water coming out of the faucet in their rooms was an odd colour. Some of them drank the water, and it tasted ghastly. Hotel maintenance worker Santiago Lopez was sent up to the roof to check the water supply. He found Elisa's body floating face-up in one of the water tanks. Fire-fighters had to cut the tank and drain it to get her body out.

The maintenance employee said that on the day he found Elisa, he took the elevator to the 15th floor and took a staircase up to the roof. He had to turn off the rooftop alarm. He said he didn't notice anything wrong with the alarm on the door to the roof that day, nor had he heard the alarm go off at any point during Lam's stay, although presumably he did not work 24 hours a day. He said he then had to climb up onto the platform where the four water tanks sat. Then, he had to climb another ladder to get to the top of the water tank. "I noticed the hatch to the water tank was open. I looked inside and saw an Asian woman lying face-up in the water."

The hotel's chief engineer Pedro Tovar, said there are four ways to get onto the roof; via 3 fire escapes through interior doors, and one staircase from the 14th floor. An alarm will sound if someone attempts to open the door to the roof. If the alarm sounds, it can be heard at the reception desk of the hotel as well as the 14th and 15th floors, he explained. 'The hotel engineer said he tested the alarm regularly,' reported CBC Canada. 'When Elisa went missing, he said it was in working order.' If someone were able to successfully elude detection somehow and access the roof, the engineer added that you would first have to climb up to the platform on which the tanks sit, then squeeze between them and an array of plumbing equipment. Once through this, you would find another ladder, which you could then use to climb onto one of the four water tanks. The engineer said in his 30 years at the hotel, he had never heard of any person being found injured or dead around or in the water towers. In fact, this was so unheard of that when the parents of Elisa Lam tried to sue the hotel for negligence, the case was dismissed on the grounds that the hotel could not possibly have anticipated that someone would get to the location in which Elisa's body was found; it just was not an easy route.

After the discovery of her body, the LA Times reported, 'Los Angeles police investigators searched the roof of the Cecil with the aid of dogs when Lam was reported missing about three weeks ago.' Homicide Detective Tennelle set up a base at the hotel in the days after Elisa's disappearance. "Every nook and cranny of the building where we thought was a room, locked or unlocked, it was to be opened – it was to be searched.' His partner, Homicide Detective Lopez however said he didn't know if the water tanks were examined by the dogs, nor all the rooms. "We did a very thorough search of the hotel," he said. "But we didn't search every room; we could only do that if we had probable cause" that a crime had been committed. Why could the police dogs not pick up her scent at all?

We know the roof could also be accessed by fire escapes that had no alarm. Would a killer have carried her up to the roof by fire escape? Would a killer have forced Elisa to climb ahead of him up a fire escape in the dark, then force her to squeeze through the gap on the ledge where the plumbing equipment was and climb up another ladder into the water tank? The detectives investigating Elisa's death, never really got to the bottom of exactly how she would have accessed the roof without triggering an alarm, if she hadn't gone via a fire escape, and yet at least one private investigator has told me that there were two possible door exits to the roof and on one of these doors, a handle was missing. Another investigator managed to access the water tower albeit via the nerve-wracking route of exiting a window and climbing the exterior fire escape ladder, and they noted at the time of filming it, that two of the water tanks' lids were actually open, though they were meant to be closed.

The homicide police believed Elisa caused her own death; that she did this to herself. "I think she went through the door," Detective Tennelle told the Cecil's lawyers. "It was my opinion that she climbed in on her own," said the Detective.

The most pertinent question really, apart from how she got onto the roof, would be why Elisa would go up onto the roof, on her own, at night, in the first place? How did she then end up inside one of the hard-to-access water tanks? Why would a slight, petite, young woman climb up one of these ladders, lift the hydraulic lid, and climb inside? Was she drugged and acting unknowingly? A date-rape drug like GHB? or Scopolamine - a drug so horrifying that you can get a person to do anything you ask them to, and they won't remember a thing about it. You can administer it very simply by casual touch or simply by blowing it at someone, and they will do anything you ask them to, then they will have no memory of what they have done. It isn't routinely screened in toxicology; although they did screen for MDMA and cocaine and found none. No illicit drugs were found in her system; unless a rare drug had been used and not been screened for in toxicology. Strangely, she had very little blood left in her body with which to carry out forensic and toxicology tests.

The lid of the water tower in which Elisa's body lay, was open when they found her. People have wondered, how did she manage to lift the large lid of the water tank? Or had it already been open when she'd got up onto the roof? It is believed that the lid was operated by a hydraulics system which would have made it easier to open, but it seems it could also quite possibly have already been open. There was however no ladder beside the water tower when her body was discovered. So how did she climb in? Or we could also say, how did she remove the ladder from the side of the water tank once inside the water tank?

No incriminating evidence was found at the scene. "It was my opinion that she climbed in on her own," Detective Tennell insisted. "My partner and I tried to figure out how somebody could have put her in there, and it's difficult for someone to have been able to do that and no leave prints, not leave DNA or anything like that." So, she climbed in on her own, he says. She was tiny, and slender. It would have been an endurance to climb up via an external fire escape ladder, then scale another ladder to get onto the platform and then climb another to get into the tank. She also would have had to find a ladder and do this in the dark, without her glasses! If she did somehow manage to do this by herself, someone could still be responsible for manslaughter - if she had been chased to her death. A review left on Yelp for the Cecil Hotel by 'Mary Kate M' says; 'SOMEONE WAS WATCHING ME SHOWER from the attached bathroom through the vent. YES, I saw someone watching me shave my damn legs through the vent! I don't know if it was an employee or a guest. Thanks a lot. I hope there isn't a video of me somewhere on the internet of me shaving my legs.'

When Elisa was found inside the water tank, she was naked. Her clothes were floating in the water. Why would she take her clothes off? There is a syndrome called 'Paradoxical Undressing,' where due to extreme cold, a person's nerves will make them begin to feel increasingly hot, and in an effort to cool down, a person will remove their clothes; but this is something that usually happens in the outdoors, such as on camping or hiking trips, when a person is ill-equipped. It's not something that is usually reported in water. Had she removed her clothes in a desperate attempt to stay afloat? Or had her clothes been removed from her body by someone else, before she entered the water? Perhaps Elisa had fled her captor nude, grabbing her clothes as she ran?

Her autopsy shows rectal prolapse. There was no suggestion she had been sexually assaulted in her autopsy report. Online Newspaper the Daily Maverik however, said they spoke to 3 doctors; "All of whom opined that the evidence was suggestive of trauma." Her autopsy said, 'The anus is oedematous and shows pooling of blood in the subcutaneous tissues surrounding the orifice.' One of the 3 doctors they spoke to said it was 'highly likely' there had been a sexual assault. Another of the doctors, Dr. David Klatzow, said there was insufficient information given in the autopsy, which made it challenging to determine what did happen to her, but he added that 'The bruising in the anus could have been a result of the body's advanced state of decomposition and have a non-traumatic cause connected to it.' A sexual assault kit was noted in the coroner's report, but no results were given, so it is likely the kit was not used. In essence then, we do not know if she was sexually assaulted, or not.

Why did she get into the water tank? In the elevator, we could suggest that her behaviour was playful; she was playing some kind of game, hide and seek let's say. Did she go up onto the roof and get into the water because she was playing a game with someone? Yet that would seem an extraordinarily risky game to play, and Elisa just did not seem that way inclined, as we shall later learn. Was this an act of suicide? - Yet there are far easier methods which spring to mind, rather than to climb up onto a roof, then climb a ladder at night, without her glasses. How would she even have known there was a water tower up there? Had she run up to the roof to escape someone, and then seen the towers and decided to hide inside one of them? That seems so dangerous, and indeed it was, because she would not emerge from the tank alive.

If Elisa had been planning to kill herself, she could simply have jumped off the roof, or out of a window; both are faster and more instant deaths than drowning. She could have taken an overdose with her prescribed medication. She had enough tablets with her to do this. Crucially however, the detectives and the Coroner did not believe she purposely tried to kill herself; they believed it was an 'accident.' But if it was an accident, what was she doing up there in the first place? And why was she naked when she was found?

Was she having some kind of nervous breakdown, a psychotic break? But why would it manifest now? She'd been taking her medication for bi-polar disorder for at least a year prior to this incident. Was she experiencing heightened anxiety, extreme internal distress, was she hallucinating or hearing voices? Hearing footsteps? Seeing shadows where no person existed? Was she fleeing something that was entirely in her own mind? Her autopsy showed she had been taking her medication but had possibly missed at least a dose of her anti-psychotic medications. Yet that surely would not have caused such an immediate and spectacular break-down? These types of medications take a while to break down and leave the system entirely.

Elisa's autopsy determined that she had drowned, with 'bipolar disorder contributing but not related to the immediate cause of death.' If she had drowned in the tank, as her autopsy says, then we know she had definitely been alive upon entering the water; unless she had been drowned in a bath or shower, and her body taken to the water tower to dispose of it. Her body had 'no trauma.' There were no signs she had fought with anyone and there were no injuries to show she had struggled to get out of the water tank. There were no scratch marks inside the water tower, and no torn fingernails. There was a ¼ inch round abrasion on her left knee. She was naked inside the water tank; her clothes were floating beside her.

What had caused this small abrasion? Had she accidentally scuffed against something with her knee during that night? Or, had she perhaps been on her knees at some point that night? Had someone forced her to her knees, in a hotel room for example? Had there been some kind of forced sexual activity that night, before she had managed to flee and escape to the roof? Why was she wearing men's shorts? Was it her fashion style? Her low-key blog 'Ether fields' was primarily a fashion blog; she was passionate about high-fashion, runway fashion, and she held dreams of becoming a full-time fashion writer. Her online posts, which we shall look at shortly, show her to be very much a follower of style, and so it calls into question why she would be wearing medium sized men's undershorts, particularly given that she was so petite. Perhaps she had been in bed, or was getting ready to go to bed and these were the most comfortable things to sleep in? Were these shorts hers?

She was a fashion blogger, but writes that she fears being judged for being too materialistic. She is also sensitive about her appearance, once commenting that though she had purchased a pair of shoes she had been dying to get, her legs looked too chunky in the photo she posted of herself wearing them. 'I have to admit I am very self-conscious about my legs. In proportion to the rest of my body, they are very thick and bulky... I shy away from dresses and skirts because my legs create a stumpy effect.' It makes one question why she was wearing unflattering over-sized men's shorts the night she vanished, but maybe they were in fashion at the time?

Along with these shorts, she wore a red hoodie and a white shirt. In the elevator of the Cecil Hotel, we can see she is wearing this outfit. Very strangely, this is identical to the outfit a character called 'Cecilia,' wore in the horror movie 'Dark Water', where a woman ends up dead in a water tower on the roof of a building. There is also a very creepy elevator scene in the movie, with a young woman dressed identical to Elisa Lam in the elevator. What happened to Elisa Lam is almost identical to this horror movie; yet the movie was made before Elisa's death. Elisa died in 2013. The movie was released in 2005. It is a remake of a Japanese horror movie made in 2002, and the story originates from a book by Koji Suzuki who also wrote

'The Rings.' The American version of 'Dark Water' stars Jennifer Connelly as 'Dahlia,' who has a young daughter called 'Cecilia.' They move into a run-down apartment.

Not long after they move in, water begins to drip from their bedroom ceiling. The elevator in the building is prone to malfunctioning, like Elisa's elevator. Cecilia sneaks up to the roof one day and finds a back-pack sitting next to the water tower. In time, Cecilia and Dahlia cannot help but notice the dark water which starts to run out of their taps and toilet. Dahlia goes up to the roof and to her horror, she finds a girl's dead body floating in the water tower; just like the real-life case of Elisa Lam at the Cecil hotel. How can it be that a movie released before Elisa vanished, seems to mimic so precisely the last known hours of Elisa's life; even down to the exact outfit she is wearing in an old elevator that malfunctions just like the elevator in the movie? Naming one character 'Cecilia,' and the other 'Dahlia,' we also cannot but help think of the infamous 'Black Dahlia' case in LA, and indeed there seems to be many similarities between Elisa Lam and the 'Black Dahlia' victim, Elizabeth Short.

Many believe that the Cecil Hotel where Elisa vanished was the last place Elizabeth Short was seen. Elizabeth Short was a young aspiring actress who was found mutilated in January 1947. Her face was carved into a 'Glasgow Smile', her body drained of blood, and cut in half, then washed in gasoline. When a local resident happened across her body, at first, they thought it was a store mannequin. Her body was left on display, deliberately to be found and seen. The notorious case of 'The Black Dahlia,' as Elizabeth Short came to be known, is an as yet still-unsolved murder-mystery that has beguiled so many. Elisa was 'washed clean' by the water, and some believe she too had been drained of blood, because there was so little blood left in her body that it was not even possible to carry out many of the necessary forensic tests. There are other striking and unsettling similarities between Elisa Lam and Elizabeth Short, whose severed body was found on Leimont Park. Both Elizabeth and Elisa were petite, brunette, and pretty, both were called names that derive from Elizabeth, both were in their twenties, and both sadly suffered from depression. Both were known to travel alone and both had travelled from San Diego to downtown LA just prior to their deaths.

Both Elisa and the Black Dahlia vanished after last being seen in a downtown hotel, and many say this was the Cecil Hotel. Both were not reported missing for a number of days before their bodies were found, and both died horrifying, inexplicable deaths that would become notorious. Both appear to have been drained of blood. Both cases 'went viral.' Newspapers around the world and armchair detectives have been fascinated with the mystery of who killed 'The Black Dahlia' for decades, and now Elisa too. Notably as already said, the movie 'Dark Water' has a central character called 'Dahlia,' and 'Dahlia's young daughter is called 'Cecilia'; so similar to the word 'Cecil,' Elisa's Hotel.

It would almost seem as though this movie ties the Black Dahlia and Elisa Lam together in a way that is impossible to explain; other than that, this was a destiny planned by a cosmic jester, having fun with us. Or, it was a plan devised and put into play by human hand, with the movie paying sick tribute to the horror of the mutilated Black Dahlia and at the same time, providing us with an exclusive preview of the terrible real-life fate to come for Elisa, who would indeed go on to end up dead in a water tower atop a building as the movie had shown us. Was this movie influenced to be made by people who knew very well what was to happen to Elisa at some point in the future? If so, who would these people be? And do their connections span aeons of inter-generational esoteric evil? Surely, that's just nonsense, isn't it? Yet, there is much more to come.

Elizabeth Short's murderer has never been found. Elisa's coroner's report noted that sand particles were found attached to her clothes. No-one knows where these came from. Her hyoid bone and larynx were intact, indicating no strangulation had occurred. There was no vaginal trauma. Toxicology determined there was 'no acute drug or alcohol intoxication.' There was limited blood available. 'Decedent had a history of bi-polar disorder for which she was prescribed medication. Toxicology studies were performed for the presence of these drugs. However, quantitation in the blood was not performed due to limited sample availability.' Had all the blood in her body seeped out of her from the ¼ inch abrasion on her leg? Or, had she been drained of blood, like 'The Black Dahlia? BBC science says: 'Because water is dense and a good solvent, fast flowing water might wash away the clotting factors before a stable clot can form on an external cut.' Was her

¼ inch cut large enough for all the blood in her body to drain out? Or had she been exsanguinated in some ghastly forbidden occult ritual? 'Toxicology results were not exhaustive due to limited blood,' the coroner's report said.

Yet, 'Police investigating did not show evidence of foul play,' says the summary prepared by the Los Angeles County coroner. 'A full review of the circumstances of the case and appropriate consultation do not support intent to harm oneself.' They determined she had not willingly committed suicide, but, 'The manner of death is classed as accident,' writes James P. Tovar, MN, associate deputy Medical Examiner. This was later changed to 'undetermined.'

The preliminary field report says that the 'original scene' was 'not disturbed.' Elisa was found in the afternoon on February 19th 2013. 'She had last been known alive on January 31st 2013 at the Cecil Hotel.' She was missing for 18 days. Her body showed 'moderate decomposition' at the scene, however, on examination at the coroner's office, she was determined to be 'in advanced state of decomposition,' and so it seems she had been dead for some time, and her clothes were 'sapping wet.' Her watch and hotel key card were also found in the water. A sexual assault kit was noted, to rule out any sexual assault; although the results were not given and it is difficult to determine if the kit was used. Her anus was prolapsed; however, this was not the result of sexual assault according to the medical examiner. A fingernail kit was used to retrieve any evidence of self-defence and any possible perpetrator DNA, but neither were found.

The criminalist report, as part of the LA County Department of Coroner Medical Examiner's report states, 'LAPD Robbery-Homicide division took the lead on her case with Det. Tennelle Stearns.' The report says, 'Video of surveillance camera in the hotel shows the decedent in an elevator at the Cecil Hotel exhibiting strange behaviour. There are no other people seen in the video and it does not appear that she is being chased or in distress,' they determine. 'She is wearing the same clothing found in the water tank.' The video is reported to be from 2/1/2013.

Detective Tennille reported, '911 and fire-fighters were called after the decedent was found in rooftop water tank by a maintenance worker when sent to check the water tanks after complaints of poor water pressure.' The coroner's report says, 'There was an unsecured metal removable hatch on the top of the tank. Clothes and shoes were found in the tank.' There had been a passage of time between her disappearance and the discovery of her body, time in which DNA could blow away, although inside the tank any foreign DNA would have surely have been trapped, one assumes. Toxicology tested for cocaine, marijuana, amphetamine and methamphetamine, MDMA, morphine, barbiturates – none were detected in Elisa; just a very small amount of ibuprofen. In her luggage, some of her prescribed medication was found. These included Advil, Lamotrigine, Quetiapine, and Venlafaxine. Many of the prescriptions had been refilled in the month prior to her death; which would seem to indicate she must have been taking her meds in the weeks prior to her death, but Elisa appeared to have possibly missed a couple of doses, at some point.

Despite there being no evidence of any person chasing Elisa according to the LAPD, the hotel seems to have been severely lacking in security cameras. Had she fled a hotel room, after being subjected to an attempted or partial sexual assault, managed to flee and got onto the roof-top to hide? Surely though, even in fear of one's life, there would have been other places to hide rather than to go up onto the roof, climb a ladder and enter the water tank, with no obvious easy way of climbing back out? Screaming while fleeing might have been more effective, and one or two guests later said they thought they heard a scream, yet any other cries for help may have been drowned out by the general noise of the hotel. Elisa was staying in a hostel-type room, however the other occupants of the room requested that Elisa be moved because she was acting strangely, and so the hotel management moved her to a private room. She had first been assigned room 506B. The hotel manager indicated that she had started leaving post-it notes on some of the other people's beds, which said, "Please leave."

The Cecil Hotel, now closed, was not a high-class expensive hotel and there had been incidents of disturbances or criminal behaviour in the past, as in any budget hotel. Police said they frequently responded to calls relating to domestic abuse and narcotics. There was much worse though; In 1964, 'Pigeon Goldie' as she was known, was found raped, mutilated and strangled to death in her room in the hotel. In 1984, serial killer Richard Ramirez 'The Night Stalker' called this hotel his home, as he conducted a murderous spree claiming 13 victims. "He was dumping his bloody clothes in the dumpster at the end of his evening and returned via the back entrance," said investigator Richard Schave. In 1991, Johann Unterwerger killed three prostitutes in his room at the Cecil Hotel.

The Cecil Hotel was once an elegant place, when it first opened, with its marbled lobby, its art deco elegance, the period chandeliers and stained-glass. With the residency of two known serial killers and the disturbingly high numbers of suicides that have taken place in the hotel; are all these negative energies, auras and emotions trapped inside the building itself? Is it a place that dark energies in the ether are naturally drawn to, to congregate and feed off? Could it be that the hotel itself is cursed? Are people drawn to this hotel as though lured to it?

Haunted Encounters television series, filmed before Elisa Lam's death, says, "There's a tremendous amount of fatalities here at the Cecil hotel. Someone has literally died in every room. In room 1121 there have been many reports of guests checked into this room feeling as if they're being physically strangled – and checking out! The things that are down in this basement are extremely powerful –

they're watching us. The basement is coming alive around us. Something big moved over there!"

Perhaps the hotel itself held the residual lingering atmosphere of death; In 1937, Grace Magro jumped to her death from a 9th floor room. The following year, Roy Thompson jumped to his death from a window on the top floor. In 1934, Louis D. Borden slashed his own throat. In 1944, the Los Angeles Times of September 8th reported 'Mother held after baby found thrown to death. After hearing testimony that one juror later described as "almost beyond belief," a coroner's juror recommended that Dorothy Jean Purcell, 19, be held to answer to a homicide charge for allegedly throwing her new-born baby boy to his death from a high window of a downtown hotel. That hotel had been the Cecil.

The LA Times reported in 2013, 'Some long-term residents told the Times five years ago that they still call the Cecil "The Suicide" because of the number of people who have jumped to their deaths from the building through the years.' The LA Times reported on June 13th 2015, after Elisa died, 'Authorities suspect a 28-year-old man who died Friday on Main Street in downtown Los Angeles may have plunged to his death from a skid row hotel, a Los Angeles County coroner's spokesman said Saturday. The man was pronounced dead Friday at 5:05 p.m. outside the Cecil Hotel, said Lt. David Smith, coroner's supervising investigator. The hotel, an 85-year-old skid row institution, operates in part as a low-budget tourist hotel and hostel called Stay on Main, but during its long and sometimes dark history was known as the Cecil. A man who identified himself as the assistant manager said the man who died was not a guest and could have been an intruder.'

Author of Gourmet Ghosts, James T. Bartlett, notes that in April 1929, Cecil hotel guest Dorothy Robinson, aged 33, was taken to hospital after being found 'in a dazed condition for three days,' after suffering from poisoning. Apparently, her husband had died a month before, and she had suffered a collapse, the drug (presumably barbiturates) prescribed for her nerves.' Also featuring 'poison,' Bartlett tells of a "James Willys of Chicago" or rather, that was the alias he used when he checked into the Cecil Hotel. The 46-year-old was really called Mr. W.K. Norton, and he came from Manhattan Beach to the Cecil hotel. He had been reported missing for a week when his body was found in his room in the Cecil hotel after he had swallowed a number of 'poison capsules.' In 1939, sailor Erwin C. Neblett drank poison in his room, as did 45-year-old teacher Dorothy Sceiger a few months later.

Bartlett also tells of the case of Benjamin Dodich, who a few months later, 'Shot himself in the head in his room,' and a Helen Gurnee from San Diego who in October 1954, 'Plunged to her death from the window of her room. She had checked in under a pseudonym 'Margaret Brown of Denver.' Her body landed on the hotel marquee and needed to be reached by ladder. Unusually, the newspaper report mentioned the room Gurnee was staying in – a detail that's usually kept back in order to prevent curious visitors – and unknowing future guests from maybe getting a ghostly surprise!' He lists the death of Julia Francis Moore, 50, who jumped to her death from her hotel room window in 1962. The Desert Sun, of October 13th 1962, reported on the death of a Mrs. Pauline Otfon, 27, who 'wrote a suicide note to her husband then leaped nine stories from the Cecil Hotel. George Giannini, 65, a transient, was struck by Mrs. Otton's hurtling body. Coroner's deputies said both were dead at the scene Friday night.'

James Edward Garcia spent 3 nights in the hotel after Elisa's death, bringing with him an EVP recorder. He believes the spirit of Elisa came through to him, while in his hotel bedroom. He asks, "Who killed you?" A voice replies, on the EVP recording, "They did." In the elevator, the same one Elisa was last seen in, he captures a voice saying; "You better keep out! Keep out!" He says, "The creepy whispering voices sound p…d. They are either warning me – or threatening me." Down in the lobby, a whispered female voice says, "James" several times. Back in his room, his recording equipment picks up what seems to be many voices; a cacophony of them. A female voice comes through, "Save me, please save me!" A man's voice says, "She died." A male voice says, "Yeah, blood." "Killing" the voice says. The female voice returns, "Please save me," to which James shouts, "Who are you?" A very deep voice replies, "They killed her," followed by a higher pitch voice saying, "A demon seed."

One night he also slept in the room serial killer Richard Ramirez called his home while on his killing spree. 'I returned to the room only to find the TV Remote on the floor with the battery cover off and a Tylenol bottle on its side on the table between the beds. I thought that Hotel

Security must have been rummaging through my room. I setup a static camera to film my night. I was not aware that my Night Shot Infrared camera picked up a skull face that had bled through the paint on the wall behind me. You can clearly see it and it is pretty scary. At one point my face seems to have morphed into some type of demon possessed creature while I was asleep. It sounds outrageous but watch the footage and you will see what I'm talking about."

Is the Cecil Hotel imbued with demons who play with those who stay there; who get inside their heads? Newsblaze reporter John Kays asks, 'Isn't it logical to postulate that whoever killed Elisa Lam (if that's what happened) was in the throes of the same evil spirit that Jack Unterweger was possessed with?' Or the spirit of serial killer Richard Ramirez? He is referring to the two serial killers who called this hotel their home. Perhaps Elisa's death had been part of a serial killer's quest; but it could just as easily have been a crime of opportunism, by a random, solitary and as yet uncaptured killer; indeed, an un-sought-after-killer too at this point and a killer-on-the-loose, because her case has been closed. Was someone covering her mouth and 'helped' her climb into the water tower? Yet police say no DNA was found at the scene. Perhaps she saw something she shouldn't have. In her blog, Elisa wrote, 'I do like people watching at the hostel.' She wrote this during her San Diego stay, but it could equally apply to the Cecil Hotel too. Maybe she was up on the roof, taking in the night-air and the sky-line of LA, feeling a bit lonely, maybe depressed, and other people were up there, up to something bad, and she saw them. She couldn't be allowed to live. And yet why wouldn't these people do whatever it was they were doing, in a room in the hotel instead of up on the roof? Perhaps it was an employee on the roof that night?

It was said that the only functioning security camera was the one in the elevator; which seems very strange, and if so, how could they know whether Elisa had been chased, or abducted? Although police dogs were brought in during the search for her after she vanished, Detective Tennelle did say they did not enter all the bedrooms – as they would have required a warrant and 'just cause.' We do not definitively know if she had been kept in a room or why the dogs did not pick up on her scent. We do not know how close to the water tower the dogs searched.

The lid to the tank was open when she was found. Would a killer have left it open? Or wouldn't they care? After all, if a killer put her body in the water tank, they knew at some point she would be found anyway; or perhaps they didn't understand that her body would affect the water in the ghastly way it did? Possibly they believed putting her in a water tank would wash away any DNA they had left on her body, and her body would not be found, and yet the two LAPD homicide detectives who went to the scene after her body was found, said there was no DNA on the tank itself – which they believed pointed to it being impossible for a perpetrator to have carried her or forced her up the ladder and into the tank without leaving any incriminating DNA behind.

Suicide victims do remove clothes. It is very common, for some reason, for those who kill themselves by wading into water, to take off their clothes before they do so. Strangely, those that do, very often also place their clothes in a neat pile before drowning themselves; but Elisa's clothes were with her in the water tower, not piled neatly outside of it.

Some believe that the elevator footage has been tampered with; approximately 1 minute is missing. Was this the police, or someone else? If it was the police, what was happening in the 1-minute cut from the footage that they didn't want us to see? Some believe the elevator has been tampered with; that her killer disabled it in some way, then played cat and mouse with her; but it was an old elevator and these are notoriously slow, laborious and unresponsive. She had pressed so many buttons that the elevator would not have responded well to this. The elevator door failed to close fast and move, because she had pressed the buttons too much. Some of her behaviour in the elevator could also be put down to her short sightedness and her missing glasses perhaps. Why was she not wearing her glasses though? Would she willingly walk around without them on, late at night, in an environment that was foreign to her? Could she see the floor numbers on the buttons she was pressing clearly enough without her glasses? We could also add, could she safely climb a 15-foot ladder on a rooftop, without her glasses, without accident?

The buttons Elisa pressed in the elevator were 14 10 7 4 B. Were these simply random, in her effort to get the elevator to respond and start moving? Perhaps it's odd that all of these numbers seem to relate to water in Bible verses from John 4. The Bible is such a large tome however, that surely verses could be plucked out that could relate to any scenario, and we are simply taking things too far now? Elisa pressed 4,7; In John 4 verse 7; 'A woman came from Samaria to draw water.' She pressed 4,10; In John 4 verse 10; 'Give me a drink.' She pressed 4,14; in John 4 verse 14; 'But whoever drinks of the water that I shall give him will never thirst. But the water I shall give him will become in him a fountain of water springing up into everlasting life.' This is all very spooky, and yet surely for it to have any real meaning, Elisa would have to have been party to it – for she was the one who pressed the elevator numbers in that sequence? And that makes no sense at all.

Her behaviour, of putting her arms out as if feeling for 'something' inside the elevator; as though a phantasm were pursuing her, could perhaps more rationally be explained by her confusion as to why the elevator would simply not close its doors and descend as she wished it to; and her hands perhaps, rather than feeling for something, were attempting to trigger the sensor she believed might be in the elevator, to make it move. Could she have been thinking the elevator was operated by infra-red, and sensitive to movement, and she was simply trying to trigger the sensors into making the elevator work faster and get the door to close? She had probably never been in such an old elevator, and perhaps she was trying to apply modern elevators to this one – her stepping in and out of the elevator and then moving to stand right in the corner of it, was perhaps her attempt to get out of the way of the sensor to get it to re-set and move. We see her poking her head out of the elevator, peering around, quickly getting back in, standing in the corner, as though playing peek-a-boo with someone, or, trying to hide from someone outside in the corridor; but what if she thought she needed to move out of the way or out of sight of an imagined sensor to activate the elevator to start working again? Did she then give up on it and take the stairs instead? Did she meet her killer on the stairs? Who would take the stairs in an hotel, for this might point to a possible suspect-type? Staff perhaps, and regulars who knew the elevator was slow and unwieldy. Or impatient, fit, youngish guests. Even a man in his fifties or sixties however, if fit, may consider walking the stairs instead of patiently waiting for an old slow elevator.

Is there also the possibility she had deliberately pressed all the buttons and was jumping in and out of the elevator because she was delaying the elevator purposely? Was she making her way down to the lobby to meet a date? Had nervous anticipation and excitement got the better of her? She was clearly shy when you read her blog, and perhaps she had pressed the buttons knowing it would buy her a few more seconds, in an effort to compose herself before she met up with her date in the lobby, perhaps a first date with someone she really didn't know, and her mind might have been full of self-questioning; "Do I look ok? Does my hair look alright? Will he like me? What will we talk about? What if it goes all wrong?" It seems that there might have been a mirror in the hotel corridor. Was she simply buying herself time, trying to compose herself to make a good impression, to make sure her hair looked ok when she got to the lobby? Was she all butterflies? She had lost her phone just prior to her disappearance, so we are not be able to track who she had been talking with or who she might have met in the days leading up to the night she vanished.

On 11.11.11, around a year before she went to LA, she had met someone. On her blog she wrote, 'Now I have a person who makes me smile deliriously. I still think it's too good to be true. I may be young but I've always thought of love to be like the ending of 'Drive.' The ending of drive is exceptionally poignant and sad. She writes, 'I feel so lucky that I met such a wonderful awesome guy. He makes what pain and anger I felt meaningless. What broken heart? Why would I ever think of killing myself? What disappointment with those I trust most? It is the feelings that I have now that has made people continue on with their lives for centuries.' – This man, a year earlier, was never mentioned again, and she was believed to be single when she arrived in L.A. Very interestingly, in this 12-month-earlier blog post, Elisa mentioned suicide, albeit dismissing it; but, a year on in LA, had her depression become too much for her? Had she even seen the movie 'Dark Water', and wanted to emulate it, by killing herself in the same way? She was a big fan of movies – mentioning 'The Great Gatsby,' and 'Terminal' in her blog, and 'Drive.' She had even intended to go to the locations where 'Drive' had been filmed. But surely, she would not have wished to inflict such a horrible death upon herself or the other guests, by dying in the same way as the victim in 'Dark Water;' her dead body seeping into the tap water? And, her pills provided the perfect suicide tool, or jumping from the roof-top. Even if she had become mentally unstable or psychotic – why go to such physical effort as to climb a huge ladder and jump into a water tank? What would even make her think of the water tank? There is nothing in Elisa's character that would even suggest she would think of anything quite so awful.

Would Elisa have climbed an external fire escape, in the dark, alone, in a fit of despair? It's possible. 'I have missed 3 weeks of class since my sleeping pattern is completely reversed,' she wrote, a few months prior to her trip to LA. 'When I cannot fall asleep at night …I am left to wander downtown…' And yet a 'wander downtown' is a little different to climbing a ladder on a roof, stripping and jumping into cold water to die. To fall in accidentally also doesn't make much sense. In her blog, she neither came across as a thrill-seeker or dare-devil. But she does show depression which is crippling at times.

In her 3rd to last blog post, on 22/3, she writes; 'I had a relapse at the start of term and had to drop 2 of the 3 courses. I feel so empty.' Her last post, on 22/4/12, reads; 'I spent two days in bed hating myself. Why don't I simply do something that I know will make me feel better? It isn't rocket science. It isn't difficult. Get out of bed. Eat. See people. Talk to people. Exercise...' It is obvious she is feeling very low here, yet this doesn't sound like the sort of person to climb onto a roof-top and climb a water tower, alone; that would need significant motivation, a significant lack of lethargy and much physical effort, although Elisa also posted this, in December 2013; 'This astonishing precipice one side of which the soul was active and in broad daylight, on the other side, it was contemplative and dark as night.' It is a quote from author Virginia Woolf, who on March 28, 1941, filled her coat pockets with rocks and walked out of her house and into the River Ouse. The depression which had followed her like a shadow in her adult life had finally caught up with her. She drowned herself.

Elisa had also posted about how her medication made her feel sometimes, particularly in her earlier days of taking it. At times she had written that her meds, when first taking them, made her feel sluggish. In 2010 she blogged, 'School has started... and it doesn't help that I can't think. I took a long unaccounted - for break from school. My brain has been sluggish. Half a year down the drain where

I did not do anything productive nor learn anything worth knowing. Now it seems my once prized organ no longer works the way it once did. I feel sluggish all day, sleepy, mopey and tired, unable to concentrate. What once came naturally is now beyond hard to grasp. I won't be able to put together a proper post for a while, then again who cares whether or not it makes any sense.'

In another post we learn much more about the way she sometimes feels, as a result presumably from taking her meds for bipolar disorder; 'I've been having headaches for the past two days and my vision shakes when I stand. I'm not sure if it's vertigo but I definitely do not feel stable even when sitting. It also gets hard to focus at times. I can't seem to process the whole scene, almost like tunnel-vision on a hand-held camera…. If only doctors worked on Sunday.' Could Elisa have been suffering the same symptoms on the night she is captured on film in the elevator? – Was her vision and sense of balance all out of sync? Is this why she was making strange hand gestures, trying to 'feel' her way in the elevator? If this is so, it would seem really strange then to imagine that she could, or would want, to make it up an external fire escape onto a very high roof, then climb up a ladder. This is not a route someone could take by accident and it's not a route someone would choose to take when they feel dizzy, nauseous, unable to focus, and shaky. It would however make someone the perfect victim; completely vulnerable and defenceless.

What more can we learn of her? Who really was Elisa Lam? We know she loved fashion and it seems she wanted to be a known writer. On 10/11/11 she wrote, 'All I'm doing is publishing writing under my own name: the thing I've wanted to do most in the world since I was six.' Interestingly, she adds, 'Why should some imagined psycho stop me from doing what I love?' But before we start thinking she is talking about a physical stalker, it becomes very clear from reading her blog, that she is not talking of someone physically following her, which of course if she had been, it would certainly have been something the homicide police could have followed-up on; but rather, she is talking online harassment, trolling, and the effect it was having on her life. Whether she had actually been trolled, she doesn't explicitly say, and her blog was not a well-known one, but her shyness and introversion and the intrusive results that can come from being public online, seemed understandably to create a perfect storm in her already stressed mind. She had a deep fear of being judged or of not being able to meet the expectation of others when she published online. She wrote under her real name, she said, and she wanted to make her own mark but it also felt overwhelming for her too. She was not a 'known' blogger with millions of followers, but even so, the pressure she felt was very tangible. She reblogged this; 'The lack of ethics and boundaries on the internet can be alarming. Trolling knows no boundaries. There is no place it won't go ... so long as they make their demonstration of power....'

On another occasion she writes, 'I think part of my reluctance, or lack of wanting, to be more pro-active on my blog is because I'm gun shy of putting myself out on the internet. It's a wonderful but scary place, full of judgement.' She also re-blogged; 'I don't ever want to feel I need to impress anyone on the internet or in real life; it's too much pressure. I don't want to feel forced to update out of fear of losing readers.' Like most young people now, creating a presence online or interacting online seems only to add more to the social pressures they may already be feeling; Are they interesting enough? Pretty enough? How many followers have they got? Elisa comes across as a charming, quirky and intelligent young lady, with the wit to question things and the self-awareness to understand who she was; mental illness and all, she was a girl who wanted to leave her own individual mark, but being online did not come naturally to her. On 22/4/12, her last post, she writes, 'I'll be judged. I can't do it. It will be a complete utter disaster and no-one will care about it and of course, the point of doing everything is to get attention and praise from other people. Yeah; I need to get the most followers and the most views. And by doing that I have to promote myself and become a phony and pander like hell. Good job you're really following all the ideals you hold so well. ... You want to be the best. The one with the best clothes, the best outfits, the best the best the best. You can't be the best. You're just a nobody, part of the crowd. You don't create anything, You don't contribute. You just stay at home and observe... You're not that special. The only thing that does make you different is that you're a complete utter failure.... God, I hate you so much.'

She is saying this to herself, starkly chastising herself because she is suffering the pressures of social media and the way the online world has replaced our reality of how the world was without it. Is it possible she simply gave up on that night in LA? - That the pressure to become someone online, amid the millions of other people attempting to do the same thing, was far too much for her ever to be able to achieve, and she couldn't take the stress, the competition, the exposure? It wouldn't be the first time a blogger or Youtuber has succumbed to the pressure. Had the competitive and critical nature of communicating in this new frontier of online interactions caused her already fragile self-confidence to fracture completely? 'I don't know how to do anything and it'll never work. I'll be judged. I can't do it.. I can't do it alone. I don't know anybody,' she wrote.

'Despite being very outgoing, I am an introvert... and have difficulty making new friends.' She is more an observer than participant. She likes to people-watch she says, when staying at the hostel in San Diego, but she is very shy. She is more comfortable in the background. She wants to be like everyone else; confident, outgoing, popular, 'followed' online, but she has a tendency to hide herself away. Much has been made in conspiracy forums of one of Elisa's tweets; it is about Invisibility. On January 13th 2013, 18 days before she disappeared, Elisa tweeted about an article published by the Huffington Post which described a Canadian company who had been awarded funding from the Pentagon to develop 'quantum stealth' camouflage for soldiers, which renders them invisible. 'Hyperstealth Biotechnology has developed "Quantum Stealth", a type of camouflage that bends light around the wearer or an object to create the illusion of invisibility.'

This camouflage creates the illusion that a person is not there; they become invisible. In that respect, a soldier, or a civilian, could truly become 'The Invisible Man;' an invisible predator, capable of stalking an unsuspecting victim, like Elisa perhaps, who would be powerless to see them coming. And where better to test such equipment than at a hotel rumoured to be one of the most haunted places in the world? A place where multiple people have killed themselves, or been murdered by resident serial killers? An invisible man was in the elevator with Elisa! We watch her floundering and grasping with her hands out in front of her, trying to feel for something that she knows is there but cannot see! But that is ridiculous, surely? "Unless you walked right into them, you wouldn't know that they were there," says CEO of Hyperstealth Biotechnology, Guy Cramer.

Why would Elisa post this tweet, given that she was not a prolific tweeter at all, and then coincidentally find herself stalked by a hunter who is cloaked in invisibility? This surely could not have been what was really happening in the elevator? This surely is too fantastical for words; although this equipment is indeed being developed and funded, by the US Pentagon. But maybe we should also consider that Elisa loved to read and she loved books, including the Harry Potter series. Maybe she was referring to how great it would be to have an invisibility cloak like the fabled 'Deathly Hallows' magical artefact, The Cloak of Invisibility, in the Harry Potter books, and so perhaps the answer to this tweet lies in Elisa's own mind. Elisa's introversion and her shyness, as noted from her blog posts, had a crippling effect on her at times. During her travels, she chastised herself for doing nothing more than sleeping and showering – telling herself she must go out the next day and see the sights. In San Diego, she wrote, 'Today I slept, took a long hot shower. It has been most productive and enjoyable. I seriously have done nothing in San Diego that is out of my normal routine at home. Now that I'm rested and well, starting tomorrow I should venture outside more.' She hid herself away from everyone.

Perhaps the fantasy of having the ability to turn herself invisible was what she was really looking for? Yet she yearned for company too; 'I feel so empty. What is the purpose of owning a nicely curated closet if there is no place to wear it? What is the purpose of reading countless articles, if there is no one to discuss it with? Ultimately, she was achingly lonely.

Poignantly and rather ironically, if anything can come out of her tragic death, it is the comfort she unwittingly gave others online, after her death, which perhaps isn't widely known. After her death, a person called Josh wrote to her on her blog; 'I'm turning 15 in a few months. Although I never would've known you, I knew we would've been great friends if our paths had crossed. The thing that disappoints me is that although there is a large age-gap, the similarity between you and me was so Unbearable. I had seen a reflection of myself. A girl that understood, that would've understood me. All we both wanted is someone there.'

Another writes, 'I'm sobbing. I'm only 14, but the thoughts you had, the emotions you felt... I understand you. I cannot believe the literal heart-ache I'm currently feeling. The loss of a soul-mate is what it feels like… And it hurts me so much to know, that now that can never happen. I don't have anyone who I thought understood me… But I know you did, and that puts me at ease… All it would've taken was a friend. Someone who would be there for you and remind you that it's ok. But it looks like that person near came. I feel so upset... Typing this, I'm not exactly sure how to feel. Happy that I found someone like me? Upset because I lost someone? I'm just ….'

Jeff wrote; 'This will seem stupid to many people, because I am writing to a dead person. I don't know you and we never met or even knew of each other's existence until your tragic fate. When I first heard of the news and saw your picture, I don't know why but I felt torn and drawn to you. ... I tried but could not let it go… Now, after reading your Tumblr's, tweets, I am at a loss for words because I feel like I am literally staring at a mirror of myself. Your words are the very words I've spoken in my life. Your fears, regrets.. I understand the cause of your depression, as it is for me… the unfulfillment of two greatest desires: to be loved, and to be understood. At times you want to be like everyone else, but inside you know you cannot be contrary to yourself. You wonder often, why is it so easy for everyone else, why is it so hard for you. I hope in death you will still be able to read this letter. Because at the very least, you would know... someone does understand you. But even in death, you have helped others. Because knowing you, now I know someone understands me. My whole life I've asked that question too... if only someone Understands what I am going through. The irony of life is that I finally found someone who does, and she is gone.'

Matt wrote, 'I too have faced a life-long sentence of crippling anxiety and depression. I too am a hermit, hiding away from the world, spending every waking hour scouring the internet for confirmation that I am not alone. ... You've touched many lives Elisa, probably even saved a lot of people too.'

On the last day of her life Elisa wrote, or rather reblogged, given the quotation marks, '"C...t again? It was odd how men used that word to demean women when it was the only part of a woman they valued." What's very strange about this is that while we could very easily interpret Elisa posting this because a man had perhaps been rude to her that day in a casual encounter; perhaps they had accidentally bumped into each other on the street, or inside the hotel and he had sworn at her? And yet, there is some graffiti that is written just beside the water tower where her body was found and it is clearly visible in the media images of the fire-fighters up on the roof by the water tower, trying to get her body out. The graffiti says; 'FEC TO CUNT HER SUMA,' which crudely translates from Latin as, 'In fact, she was a C…t' A similar graffiti tag was also found not far from the tower, with the additional letters '2012.' Was the graffiti written there prior to Elisa's death? Again, this is probably just another coincidence… and yet there are so many coincidences in Elisa's case, and each one seems laden with such explicit symbolism; For example, Elisa Lam was a student at the University of British Columbia, although she had taken time out from her studies and was not actively enrolled at the time she visited L.A. However, her University has a Centre for Tuberculosis Research. When Elisa Lam vanished in Downtown LA, there was, at exactly the same time, an outbreak of strain-resistant Tuberculosis. In fact, the outbreak happened right beside the Cecil Hotel, on 'Skid Row.'

Strangely, one of the most widely used Tuberculosis diagnostic tests for rapid detection is called 'LAM-

ELISA.' How odd that Elisa Lam, at the time of her disappearance, would share the same name as a TB test which could be used for the TB outbreak that was happening exactly where she was located. How could this possibly be? And why? Surely, it is simply just uncanny; but there is much more to come… Perhaps we should also note that an anagram of Elisa Lam is I AM SEAL. The 'Seven Seals' in the Bible saw the arrival of the Four Horses of Apocalypse from the Book of Revelation. It tells of a scroll held in God's right hand, sealed by seven seals. The Lamb, with Elisa's surname being, of course, LAM, opens the first four of the seven seals, which summons four beings who ride out on horses. The first Horseman, who rides out on a white horse, is often referred to as 'Pestilence,' and represents infectious disease or plague; such as Tuberculosis. Evangelist Billy Graham also interpreted the first Horseman as the Antichrist.

While 'Skid Row,' next door to the Cecil Hotel in L.A. was experiencing a 'plague' outbreak, across the pond in London England, another Cecil Hotel once stood along The Strand. In marked comparison to the budget accommodation of Elisa Lam's Cecil Hotel, the London Cecil Hotel was the epitome of luxury and refinement.

It was built in 1886 with stone and red brick, as a high class and very expensive luxury hotel. It had a built-in masonic hall. It was at this Cecil Hotel that one of the most infamous men in England, Aleister Crowley; known as 'The Beast,' or 'the Wickedest man in the world,' took up residence in 1889. In 'The Confessions of Aleister Crowley,' we know Crowley 'took a room in the Cecil, and busied myself with writing on the one hand and following up the magical clues on the other. Jephthah, and other poems, were written about this period. It is a kind of backwater in my life... I was the more ready to be swept away by the first definite current. It was not long before it caught me.'

Crowley was introduced to George Cecil Jones, a member of the Hermetic Order of the Golden Dawn at this Cecil hotel, and through Cecil Jones, Crowley was introduced to the Book of the Sacred Magic of Abra-Melin the Mage. At this Cecil hotel, Crowley was initiated into the Outer Order of the Golden Dawn by its leader Samuel Liddell MacGregor Mathers and here at the Cecil hotel he wrote the work 'JEPHTHAH – Collected Works vol. 1.' He begins with a dedication quoting Il Penseroso, a poem by John Milton, (of Paradise Lost.)

'Let my lamp, at midnight hour,

Be seen in some high lonely Tower

And of those Daemons that are found…..'

Some think this is a foreboding and oblique reference to the tower in which Elisa was found drowned at the other Cecil Hotel, in L.A. In the poem, the character 'Jeptha' is a judge, who is featured in the Hebrew Bible and in the Pseudo-Philo works, an ancient biblical text. This judge offered his daughter as a willing sacrifice. His daughter was called Seila; which happens to be an anagram of Elisa. Was Elisa someone's 'willing sacrifice' in the 'high lonely tower'? Was there some great occult meaning, revealed in plain sight, in the ritual of the drowning death of Elisa Lam?

In his 'Jephthah' book, Crowley also writes an 'invocation' of a spiritual resurrection; 'Then rose thy spirit through the shaken skies; "Child of the Dawn, I say to thee, arise!... Let there be light! – the desecrated tomb Gaped… The stone rolls back: the charioted night… The splendid forehead, crowned with Love and Light… Now Freedom, flower and star and wind and wave And spirit of the unimagined fire... may seek her sire... In the pure soul of Man, her lips may have... In the pure waters of her soul's desire, Truth: and deep eyes behold thine eyes as deep, Fresh lips kiss thine that kissed her soul from sleep.'

Another allusion to water again? But of course, poems are often simply metaphorical, and it may be that Crowley was referring to political strife at the time and the fight for freedom from the 'system.'

According to Thelema, a set of magical, mystical and religious beliefs formed by Crowley, in his 'Amalantrah Workings' of 1918, a magick ritual he devised and conducted apparently led to the physical manifestation of a channelled entity. Crowley claimed he had opened up a cosmic portal through this high magick ritual, and out came this creature. This inter-dimensional entity, which was later drawn in a sketch by Crowley and looked remarkably like the later drawings of 'Gray aliens,' Crowley named it 'LAM.'

Perhaps it may also be interesting to note that Elisa Lam was born on April 30th. This is Walpurgisnacht, or 'Walpurgis Night' – the night of the Witch, sometimes also called Beltane, but most commonly known as May

Day. We may picture the innocent custom of dancing round Maypoles, but the ancient Druids would sacrifice a human at this time, to appease the gods and hope for good harvest. These days, we have an effigy instead of a human being; the burning man. On Walpurgisnacht in ancient Germanic folklore, a Harlequin figure leads an army of ghosts and lost souls. The harlequin is the leader of the involuntary dead. He is depicted as a black-faced emissary of the Devil. He roams the countryside under the dark of night with his band of demons, seeking the souls of people to carry them to Hell. In 1091, a monk called Walkelin claimed he witnessed 'The Wild Hunt.' 'An enormous tree-trunk was being carried by two men, on which was strapped and bound "some wretch tightly trussed, suffering tortures." A fearful demon was sitting astride the same tree trunk. The demon was sticking "red-hot spurs" into the man's loins. This was undoubtedly the Hellequin's Army, doomed souls marching through the land.'

Walpurgisnacht is the highest day on the Druidic Witch's calendar, and as midnight strikes, May 1st is supposedly one of 'the Illuminati's' most sacred holidays – a human sacrifice is demanded at this time, it is said. But Elisa didn't die on Walpurgis Night, she was born on it. Does this render it a useless fact? Most probably, and yet one confidential source I spoke with, who pointed this fact out to me, and who had been working as a private investigator on the Elisa Lam case, also pointed out to me that there was another very strange death of a young woman not too far away from L.A. This young woman had also been displaying very strange and irrational behaviour on the night of her disappearance, like Elisa had in the elevator, and she too ended up dead not long after, though it took some time for her to be found, but it is most likely that she died in water too. This young woman was also born on Walpurgis Night.

I first wrote about the Elisa Lam case back in 2014 in my book 'Something in the Woods is Taking People,' and talked about it on my first appearance on Coast to Coast AM in 2015. I was interviewed on a podcast a year or so later and was asked about the Elisa Lam case again. After the show had aired, it was posted on YouTube and a person posted a comment below it with a link to a video they had made; about the most remarkable discovery in this case. The video they had made went on to explain that the i.p. privacy registration of the website for 'The Last Bookstore' in LA; the last place Elisa was known to have been at on the day of her disappearance; this had been done through a company that had the exact same ZIP code as her grave.

'The Last Bookstore's' website privacy registration had been done through this company prior to Elisa Lam's disappearance. It was registered on 19/08/2009. Elisa disappeared in January 2013. I checked and this registration was not tampered with or altered after her death; it was filed before her death. The funeral home of Elisa Lam; Forest Lawn Funeral Home in Vancouver, has the ZIP code of V5G3M1. The company used by 'The Last Bookstore' to register their website privacy, also has the exact same ZIP code; V5G 3M1. While this company of course registers thousands of other companies' websites' privacy; there are also thousands upon thousands of website domain privacy companies that 'The Last Book Store' could have chosen to use to register their website privacy with. Instead of any of these thousands of other companies, 'The Last Book Store,' prior to Elisa's death, chose to register it with a company that has the exact same ZIP Code as the cemetery where her body now lies. 'The Last Bookstore' featured quite predominately in the media coverage of the search for Elisa, as it was the last place she was known to have been alive before she was captured on footage in the elevator of the Cecil Hotel. Their website indirectly points to the exact spot where her dead body now lies. How could this even be possible?

Once more, the riddles surrounding Elisa only seem to get more puzzling; with yet another seemingly impossible coincidence. The person who sent the message to me about this coincidence after my video was aired on YouTube, called themselves 'Jesper.' A curious google search of the name 'Jesper,' took me to the first result on google – it was an article on Tuberculosis; once again forming some kind of loop back to the tuberculosis outbreak beside the Cecil Hotel and the LAM-ELISA test. Perhaps the person was well-aware a google search would lead me there and had purposely created this user name of 'Jesper.' It sounds almost like 'Jester,' doesn't it? And so, the games continue…

The advertising poster for the movie 'Dark Water' says 'Dark Water conceals darker secrets.' The tag-line for the poster says; "Some mysteries were never meant to be solved…." Why was Elisa's fate played out in this movie so precisely, as though it was pre-destined? Who were the two men that came into the lobby of the Cecil Hotel and handed Elisa Lam a box? What was in that box? Was Elisa Lam 'Alice in Wonderland?' Alice cries, her tears flood the hallway, Alice swims through her tears ...she meets characters who do nothing but tell her riddles. Elisa went to 'The Last Bookstore,' Elisa met two unknown men who gave her a mystery box. Was she hunting but became the Prey? Did her killers play cat and mouse with her? Did she become the sacrificial Lam?

## Chapter Three:

# The strange disappearnce of Donald

"A New York advertising man's disappearance from a desolate Wyoming highway has all the ingredients of an intriguing mystery novel - except for the final chapter," The Observer Newspaper said, on April 12th 1984.

The reason they said this, is because the final chapter is unable to be written. The mystery itself has not been solved, and it's a complex web of cryptic clues that despite the passing of more than 30 years, remain ever elusive.

His Mother once said, "This is a horror." His sister said, "It was all my fault that we ever went to that house in Maryland. I'm sorry I ever suggested it.... I don't know what everything means. It's all so weird.... The story is so much more bizarre than I told at the time."

It's the most intriguing, baffling and mystifying true story, which encompasses elements of a Presidential assassination, seances, doppelgangers, cover-ups, robberies, ghosts, and the deaths of anyone connected to it, and of course, the disappearance and unexplained death of her brother, Don. "This all started because of a séance at that house, and everything went crazy from there. I still don't like to think about that night," his sister said. But there was much more to it than that.

It was November 1982, and her brother Donald Kemp was working in New York City at an advertising agency. Outside of work however, he was a passionate researcher into Abraham Lincoln. In particular, he was most interested in the circumstances surrounding the president's assassination. So much so, that he belonged to a group who shared their obsession for Lincoln, and indeed he had spent much time on his own private research too, with the intention of writing a book about it.

Don had only recently partially recovered from a traffic accident, and it was believed that he had been left with permanent injury as a result of it. Whether it was as a consequence of his slow recovery from this accident, as some have theorized, that led him to abandon the rat-race of New York City and take off for the wilds of Wyoming, in search of tranquillity and respite; or whether, as he told his friends, he'd made the decision to go out of the city because he intended to finally write his book on Abraham Lincoln and the events that surrounded his assassination, we cannot be sure. Don had been researching it for many months and he had amassed an enormous amount of paperwork and notes with which he was to construct the book, and certainly some of his friends and family believed that was why he had headed there, to that desolate place.

He left New York City with his car packed full of his belongings, and headed West. On his journey, he stopped off at a museum in Cheyenne on November 15th, 1982. He reportedly spent a couple of hours there, leaving without realizing he had left behind his briefcase.

The next night, his vehicle was found abandoned with the engine still running, on a remote road in a Wyoming prairie, about 40 miles from the nearest town. Don was no-where to be seen. The doors were open, and a trail of clothing was strewn across the road. A set of footprints in the snow appeared to indicate that he had walked away across a field.

After his vehicle was reported to local law enforcement, a search was initiated immediately. A duffel bag was discovered some distance from the car, containing items that were later identified as belonging to Don, and rather strangely, three of his socks were found 6 miles away in a barn, lying next to a pile of wood which appeared to have perhaps been gathered in order to build a fire. Due to a snow blizzard, the search for Don had to be abandoned after 3 days.

During the search, local law enforcement said they found no other tracks in the snow apart from a single trail of footsteps. They covered the area by helicopter too, but again found nothing that would indicate anyone else had been there, but neither could they find any trace of Don. Though they had found the footprints, the footprints did not lead anywhere. The trail of footprints very oddly appeared to simply just stop after a short distance. They ended in the middle of no-where. How could his footprints just stop like that? Where did he go? How could he have gone anywhere without leaving more footprints?

The missing man's family asked the local Sheriff if a search could be carried out using tracker dogs, but the sheriff said this would not be possible now, perhaps because of the blizzard conditions that had set in during the search for Don. The police believed the missing man had to have died out in the harsh conditions; although the bad weather only set in a couple of days after Don's disappearance.

Don was not in the barn where they found 3 of his socks, and he was not out anywhere on the snow-covered prairie. Crucially, although a blizzard did come, it had not been snowing at the time his car was found abandoned; the snow arrived three days later.

Five months later, two separate individuals came forward to say they had seen him in Casper, Wyoming, and in Cheyenne. Then, a close friend back in New York City received several missed calls. She was out of the city when the calls were made to her apartment, but an ansaphone message had been left for her, and when she returned and listened to the messages, she heard Don's voice; or at least, she was absolutely sure it was his voice.

The police managed to trace the phone number that these calls had come from. They were traced to a trailer in Wyoming. The young male resident of the trailer was a man by the name of Mark Dennis. Unfortunately, he claimed to have no knowledge of the calls ever having been made, despite them appearing on his phone bill.

The local Sheriff questioned him several times about these calls. The man denied having made them. The Sheriff said he felt satisfied with this. The missing man's mother however, was not satisfied. She questioned the young man too, most insistently, determined to get the truth, but again, the man in the trailer said he was not able to tell her anything, or perhaps the man was not prepared to. The police though, said they did not have enough reason to obtain a search warrant for his home. The young man sought out the service of a lawyer, and later, moved away from the area entirely.

It was to be four long years later that Don's mother was able to have closure; or was she? Her son's body was found, four years later, not far from the spot in which his car had been found abandoned. His body was in pristine condition. It was suggested that he had died of exposure, not long after his unexplained disappearance.

So, perhaps it was a simple but tragic case of a man's unplanned disappearance, due, as some have theorized, to some kind of nervous breakdown, which caused him to evacuate his car in the middle of no-where and walk off into the distance to inevitable death in the cold climate of Wyoming. The thing is, the story isn't so cut and dried. It really isn't a story that can be given an easy ending, because it leaves an array of cryptic unanswered questions.

In completely unprecedented circumstances, his body had not attracted any natural predators; no animals or vultures had been drawn to his dead body. There was no way that his body had been covered by snow for 4 years – the snow would have melted; and, it hadn't been snowing the night he disappeared nor for two further days. Also, his footprints didn't lead anywhere. Where they stopped, there had been no body: and the authorities had looked there for 3 days! When he'd disappeared, he also wasn't seen anywhere during the search. There had been no sign of him whatsoever.

His friend, Judy Aiello, now a well-known artist in New York, had been Don's co-worker for ten years prior to his disappearance. She knew his voice well. She said that she received 5 calls from him to her phone line, while she was away. On February 27th 1983, she received two phone messages on her ansaphone. Two more on April 5th, and another one five days later. Don's mother said, "She recognized his voice. She said my son spoke in a strained, urgent voice and gave a number where he could be reached."

The artist's number was unlisted. She could not be called without someone already knowing her number. The question is, how could Don have made the call, when the cops believed he had died very soon after he'd disappeared? His backpack was found soon after his abandoned car was found; did someone else call her? Someone pretending to be him? Why would they do that? Was it a prank? Was it the guy from the trailer who said he had never met Don? Or, had someone else stolen his backpack?

His sister wonders, "Did this man come across my brother's body and take his possessions including his phone book?" And this is where it gets weird. "This man looked very, very similar to my brother. I looked in high school pictures; they could have been twins. Did this person kill my brother, and take his personal things? Or, could it have been a case of mistaken identity because they looked so alike? They were practically doppelgangers." What are the odds that Don would disappear in the middle of nowhere only for the single lead to point them to a doppelganger of Don?

When the artist returned to New York, she heard the messages and called the number he had left on the ansaphone. A man picked up, and when she asked to speak to her friend, he said, "Yes," followed swiftly by "No," and then hung up. It was the man who lived in the trailer; the man the missing man's mother believed had to be involved. Online over the years, people have put forward the idea that her son was secretly gay and had been experimenting with his sexuality with this man. His sister however, responded to these allegations by stating that he had been a well-liked and handsome man who had been very popular with the ladies. "Don was most certainly not gay. He was very much a ladies' man, and, he was engaged." She described him further as "He was magnetic, and extremely intelligent."

While the Sheriff, Captain Mark Benton said that his investigation into the man in the trailer was "Inconclusive," he also did not pursue the matter further, believing he had nothing to go on. He said the man "implied someone else made the calls from his trailer without his knowledge," but the Sheriff couldn't confirm or disprove this.

The deceased man's mother felt the investigation lacked thoroughness, particularly with regards to this man, and noted that her son's car was not fingerprinted, nor were casts made of the footprints that led away from the car.

The police appeared to be quite keen to go along with the conclusion that her son died of exposure, because presumably they felt they had little else to go on. They were keen to push the theory that Don had suffered some kind of mental breakdown and walked away across the Prairie in a protracted act of suicide. Yet his footprints had mysteriously and inexplicably simply stopped; and his body had not been there when they'd looked for him. The victim's sister, as well as his mother, were not of the opinion that this was a suicide at all. His mother believes he was abducted by the male who lived in the trailer, or perhaps a different male/or males and that he was held prisoner in the trailer, then killed. If that were the case however, why were his socks found in a barn 6 miles from the scene of his abandoned car, along with a pile of fire wood?

The alternatives to the explanation that he abandoned his own vehicle and walked away to certain self-inflicted death, is that he was abducted. The problem with this of course lies in the lack of a second trail of footprints, although some sleuths have suggested that an abductor, holding a gun to the back of Don's head, could have stepped in the same footprints as Don to conceal his own. The abductor would have to have walked with a great deal of confidence and carefulness to have succeeded in doing this, and the barn was 6 miles from the abandoned car. Perhaps it's still possible, but it's also very far-fetched to imagine. Perhaps there were only 3 socks found in the barn because the 4th sock had been pushed into Don's mouth to keep him quiet.

There has never been an official explanation about the socks, the missing footprints, the phone calls, which could not have been a mistake on the part of the phone company; the calls were itemized on the trailer occupier's phone bill. Had Don been abducted then, and held at this man's trailer? But how did his body come to be found in pristine condition and so very close to the scene of his disappearance; yet 4 years after his disappearance? Locals in Wyoming at the time expressed the strangeness of the circumstances. They didn't think his body would have been left alone by the natural predators out there, and the harsh weather too, they said, would have taken its toll on his body before it was found, even if it had been frozen and hidden under snow. Also, how could a body lie out in the open for so long and not be noticed, if, as the police had believed, he had been there all that time? Even though it was a remote location, the land had to be owned by someone? He disappeared when it wasn't snowing, so he couldn't have been buried by snow. Would the land owners have left their land unchecked for 4 years? If Don had killed himself, or been killed, his body would have been there, and it surely would have been found?

Had he been abducted by someone who had blocked his path on the road? - Someone with another vehicle, who had flashed their lights at him to make him stop, or placed a hazard in the road which forced him to stop? Did someone pretend to be a distressed person in need of his help? If so, why would one set of footprints lead away and then just stop? Why would he have been placed back in the same spot 4 years later, after he had been killed? How was his body discovered in a condition that was completely unmarked and untouched?

As Don's footsteps were the only ones found, had he fled from someone or something? Had he run, in a desperate attempt to get away from someone or something? He was in the middle of no-where. What are the chances a random robber or kidnapper chose to assault him at that spot? How would they know anyone would be coming along that quiet road? Or, maybe they had followed him. Maybe they were following him for a while and specifically wanting him. Of course, if that had been the case, there is still the mystery of the 1 set of footprints that led away from the car and then stopped.

None of it makes any sense at all. His sister has much more information however; but it leads in an entirely different direction and one that is incredible to say the least. After her brother's death she says, "An expert professor from the Smithsonian Institute in Washington, Dr. Angel, called and asked for my brother's remains. We approved it and his body was sent there to him. This doctor said that my brother's body was in perfect condition; untouched, and he concluded that there was no way he had been laying in the open for the last 3 years. It was unheard of, he said it couldn't have happened; not with wolves, bears etc. So much has occurred that wasn't known but it is beyond bizarre. Some happened before his death; some happened after his death."

The doctor was a consultant to the F.B.I. and an expert in anatomy and anthropology. "How did this Doctor at the Institute even hear about my brother? What made him contact us? Why did he want to see my brother's body? This Dr told us that his body was totally untouched, and that he had been dead no longer than 1-2 years. There was something else very, very strange. I know it was my brother's body because he verified other injuries he had sustained before in his life. Then he told me that his hyoid bone (the U-shaped bone in the neck which supports the tongue) was missing and there was a small perfectly round hole in his head. He was insistent that nothing he knew of was capable of causing that hole. He said he had never seen anything like it. While he said that his body was in perfect condition; he meant it was mummified. I'm just repeating what was said to me."

"Before my brother left for Wyoming, he had given me a book. It was about the Universe. He turned to a page that said, 'The Pleiades,' and he said, "I don't know why, but I feel this may be of some importance. You may need this later."

In the same area that my brother disappeared, before we found Don's remains there, there was a U.F.O. group run by a Dr. Springer. They said they were there because of some cattle mutilations. One member of this group phoned me and they told me that they believed "they" - a U.F.O.? had taken my brother. This story is so much more bizarre than I told at the time. They told us they had been camping out in this area due to cattle mutilations and my brother had been 'taken.' They were camped out the night my brother went missing, they said they were researching some cattle mutilations. They called me a couple of years later telling me things. I dismissed them as being off the wall; but after we found my brother and the Smithsonian Doctor told us his findings, I didn't know what to think. I also wondered, years later, how Dr. Angel heard about Don's case; it hadn't been on the TV yet." This was before the internet and social media. It was also before Paranormal and 'Alien' shows started appearing as mainstream shows on T.V. "At that moment, (when contacted by the UFO groups) I didn't believe things could get any more insane; then, all that time later, when they found my brother's body and the Dr. at the Smithsonian examined the body, in his report, and what he told me, was that he was completely puzzled over both how the body was so preserved, and how the hole had been made in his skull."

"If my brother had just walked out of his vehicle, had a mental breakdown, then how did that account for this Doctor's findings? Was he killed because someone thought he knew something; something related to U.F.O.'s? - This was two decades before all the Ghost Hunters and UFO TV shows. How did this have something to do with UFO's? He went missing in the same area as cattle mutilations. His body was mummified. The hole, according to the Doctor was not caused by any animal nor by any known instrument. He told me he had never seen anything like it."

"I had put the book he'd given me on my book-shelf and had forgot all about it as soon as he'd given it to me. The UFO group who'd been camped out in the area and who later contacted me, said they felt that whatever "They" were out there looking for, "They" came from a place called "The Pleiades." - The same word Don told me I might need to know!"

"When the Doctor attempted to replicate the wound, he found it impossible. When my brother first went missing, we had calls from lots of U.F.O. people but I just dismissed them all. Then came the Doctor's mystifying findings. What was his interest in the case? I know it all sounds crazy and yet I am talking about the facts.... Then there is also something else which plays its part in this story. Something happened before all this. It was all my fault that we ever went to that house in Maryland. I'm sorry I ever suggested it.... I don't know what everything means. It's all so weird. My brother had already done years of research into Lincoln when we visited Surratt House Museum in Maryland. There was a woman at the reception and when we went in, she asked us if my brother was the man writing the book. When he said, "Yes," she said she had been told by someone to give him their name and phone number. I hesitate to talk about this because it unsettles me still, but my brother contacted the person and it turned out to be a young lady. She said she was a psychic and she wanted him to come to a séance. She told him she had been "contacted" in regards to the assassination of the President. He said it would be fun to go to and that he couldn't pass that up."

"So, one night we went to her house. He brought his best friend and there was a group of us altogether, including her husband, and we sat around this lady's dinner table. In the centre was a Ouija board. My brother had brought with him a tape recorder and he set up a camera to record anything that happened. We began, and the psychic began to ask questions out loud, and the planchette started to move. She then began speaking in a strange voice, speaking with words that were very antiquated; words that we do not use now. She also said things she couldn't have known; unusual names she could not have any prior knowledge of, but that were relevant to us. Some of her knowledge frightened me because she couldn't have known it. Then she began choking and I could see a red line forming across her neck. The room became freezing and the camera began to flick its lights on and off. In the flashing of the camera I could see the shadow of what looked like a woman in the hallway. It looked like she had a long dress on with a bustle in the skirt. The room became colder than ever and it felt as though evil had entered the room."

"The room became loud; I know because my brother had to shout over everyone to be heard. I don't know why but there was chaos in the room, and he shouted at everyone to get away from the table. He got us all together and he said the Lord's Prayer out loud. I guess he didn't know what else to do, but gradually everything returned to normal again. After that, I never went to a séance again, but I know my brother did because he stayed in contact with this psychic. I know it's easy to dismiss this and laugh it off, but I know this was not just hysteria; I was there when it happened. I know what I saw, and I know what I felt and I would never want to have that experience again. A lot more happened after this, but I removed myself from it. That evil, whatever it was, it was palpable."

"My brother had done years of research among the archives on the assassination. He told me he had uncovered something very disturbing, but he didn't tell me exactly what it was; he didn't specify. Did Don discover something and did someone know he had found something? Or, did they think he had found something? Perhaps it was all coincidence, but I don't know how else to explain all the robberies and break-in's and deaths."

In 1983, Don's mother asked one of Don's friends if he would go to Wyoming and drive back her son's car. The friend took a plane and went to claim the car, then began the drive back to Maryland. The vehicle was broken into when he parked it overnight in a motel as he slept. Many of the dead man's research papers were stolen. While parked at the airport, it was broken into again. When the car was returned to the family in Maryland, it was broken into once more, and further personal items relating to his research was taken. When the remaining items were put into storage, another theft occurred. Now, almost all of his independent research on the assassination had been taken.

Some of the remaining papers were given to a historian, who died very soon after in a traffic accident. A few audio tapes remained, which had not been in storage or in the car. The family donated these to a man called Mr. Frank Carrington in Virginia. Soon after taking possession of the audio tapes, his house was burnt down with him in it and he died. Other papers which the family still had, were donated to a Civil War store.

According to Don's sister, "The owner of the store died in an accident, and the papers were no-where to be found. Once all of his research had been destroyed or taken, all of the break-ins and accidents, stopped."

Don's friend says that when he arrived back at his own home and parked the car outside, he found two coins on the floor. One was face up and had been made in the year his friend had been born. The other was face down and had been made in the year his friend had vanished. Perhaps that was simply a coincidence; but Don's friend said, "He had a thing about coins. He would say if you find one face up it's good luck. If you find one face down, it's bad luck. As the years have passed, I've continued to see coins when I travel and almost all of them are from the year he disappeared. How do I explain that? I continue to have experiences where I feel he is trying to tell us all something from the afterlife."

Was Don Kemp's family being fed disinformation about "UFO's" and "cattle mutilations" to divert their suspicions that Don had been silenced because of the information he had said he'd uncovered about the President's assassination? And yet, the assassination happened so long ago, was it really that sensitive if a revelation came out? If it was proof that the official version of the assassination was not the correct one, then perhaps it was. If it was a disinformation campaign however, how did that explain the unidentified wound in his skull, and the paranormal happenings?

Had Don staged his own disappearance? Had he fled and been hiding out in the barn? Had he been abducted and held prisoner? Why was the Sheriff so reluctant to bring in search dogs? What had his doppelganger in the trailer to do with his disappearance and death? Had Don made the phone calls himself, in an attempt to seek help from someone? Where had his body been for the years it had been missing? How had it become mummified? Why could experts not work out how the hole in his skull had been made? What had he uncovered in his research about Abraham Lincoln's assassination that appears to have resulted in a number of people's mysterious accidents and deaths?

## Chapter Four:

## I'm a freak

"I'm a freak. I have hands and I have feet, and if you saw me, you'd faint, you'd be petrified, mummified, turned into stone."

These were the words of 'Gef', the strangest entity, that bewildered a farming family and most of the United Kingdom when his story was reported on across many city newspapers.

"It is impossible to deny that there is serious evidence ... for Gef's reality," said Mr. R.S. Lambert of the BBC, in the 1930's. We could be forgiven for believing that Gef was a man, or a boy, but in fact 'Gef' was an animal, an animal that appeared not quite of this world.

The closest description of 'Gef' or 'Jeff' was apparently a

mongoose. That could talk. Mongoose is the English name for family of Herpestidae, who are small carnivores native to Eurasia, Africa, and Southern Europe. They have long bodies, long angular faces and short legs with a tail. They were venerated in ancient Egypt for their ability to handle venomous snakes. 'Gef,' who was most colloquially called 'Jeff,' also took on other appearances too – varying from a strange cat, to something that looked a bit like a pig, and other indefinable small monsters.

Mostly though, Geff was invisible. He appeared on the Isle of Man at a small and isolated farm called Doarlish Cashmen, owned by 58-year-old Mr. T. Irving, a former travelling piano salesman. Mr. Irving himself was somewhat of an anomaly, for although he owned the farm, he did not work it and remained always immaculately suited with uncalloused hands.

He and his wife had a 12-year-old daughter called Voirrey, who was known to wander the Moors alone except accompanied by her dog Mona. It was said that the dog would hypnotise a rabbit with mesmerism while the child sneaked up on the rabbit from behind and clubbed it to death!

The Isle of Man Newspaper wrote: 'The spook or buggane has chosen an ideal spot. No lonelier place could be found …isolated from the outside world ..up a narrow lane. The buggane as we shall call this creature has set aflame the fumes of fancy; an evil spirit has taken possession.

The family's farmhouse was up a steep desolate hill and two miles from the nearest village. It was a small affair with no running water and no electricity. It had stone walls and small windows and it was lined with thick wood panelling on the inside. This gave the house some insulation from the cold winds and there was a gap between the walls as a result of the panelling. The story of Geff began when the family started hearing coming knocking from inside of the house.

Not only were there knocks coming at all hours, but there seemed to be no explanation for what could be causing the knocks. It was not the sound of rats or mice scurrying around. It was not anyone knocking on the walls from outside – for the father checked repeatedly and never found anyone standing outside of the house.

It wasn't just knocking though – there was wild and terrifying growling, barking, gurgling sounds, and even more strangely, frequent blowing sounds. At other times it sounded like a gurgling baby trying to say its first words. These odd bodily noises began to be heard at all hours of the day and night, and yet the family could find no source to explain where the animal sounds were coming from.

In an endeavour to try to solve the mystery of the puzzling noises, Mr. Irving decided to make noises against the walls himself. To his surprise, whatever noises he made, whether grunts or gurgles, the same noises came back at him from behind the wood panelling. Then it began spitting at them.

Very disturbed by this, and concerned for the safety of his wife and daughter, Mr. Irving set a number of traps, in an attempt to catch the perpetrator, whatever it turned out to be, although he could not for the life of him understand how barking, growling, spitting and even giggling could be coming from the tiny spaces between the walls and the wood panelling – the gap was certainly not big enough to host any animal large enough to growl.

Nevertheless, he set a number of traps and laid down poison to catch the creature. This had no effect however and proved entirely fruitless. The noises continued unabated. Some nights it kept them awake until 3 a.m. with incessant chatter.

In exasperation one day, Mr Irving exclaimed, "What in the name of God can he be?" To which he received the reply, or rather a voice, mimicking him. "What in the name of God can he be?" came the voice back at him, in falsetto tone, an octave higher than a woman's voice.

After Mr. Irving recovered from his shock, he decided to carry out some experiments with whatever creature remained hidden behind the panelling. For a start, he began reciting come of his daughter's nursery rhymes. The creature responded by reciting them back to him, word for word. It was even capable of reciting the rhymes backwards, perfectly, with no difficulty at all. It would sing the nursey rhymes too, as though it had always known them, completely fluently.

The creature announced that it had always been able to talk, but that it had started with animal grunts and growls to get the family acclimatised to its presence! "It announces its presence now by calling myself or my wife by our Christian names," said Mr Irving.

The creature apparently most liked being in the ceiling rafters above the stairs. Its voice seemed most often to come from there now. Yet the family still could not visibly see it at all. Then it began to mimic the family's conversations, reciting them back to the family. No matter where in the house the family talked to each other, the creature appeared to be able to hear them and parrot it back at them. Even when the family whispered to each other, astoundingly, the creature repeated everything they whispered, back to them.

With still no idea what this creature looked like, Irving said, "It's hearing powers are phenomenal. It is no use whispering. It detects the whisper 15-20 feet away, tells you that you are whispering, and repeats it exactly."

Not only that, but Geff seemed to have an uncanny ability to tell them gossip that would later turn out to be true. Geff said that he often left the house and travelled on the bus or in the backseat of cars belonging to the other Islanders, and he heard things on his travels. He would tell them all manner of private things, which in time would come out in gossip from the other residents of the Island, and what he told them would always be scandalously correct.

As time went on, Geff eventually allowed the family to 'feel' him. On a few occasions, he allowed them to put their hand up through the ceiling rafters and touch his fur. He even let them feel his tiny sharp teeth once. They gave him food – bacon, sausages, and chocolate; but he would not eat their eggs. For some reason he just didn't like them!

In kind, as a gesture of gratitude to the family, he would kill rabbits in the fields for them and leave them to be found. He apparently preferred to kill them with his bare hands! By strangulation. The Manx Newspaper said, 'He has been seen in many forms and resembles many animals. With the body of a weasel or a cat, and a pig's head with great glowing eyes, hissing breath and a high-pitched voice.'

Although it seemed that Geff was intending no harm to the family, and seemed to be simply a playful prankster, it must have been a little alarming to find the strangled rabbits. When he'd first made his appearance known in the farmhouse, Mr. Irving had been concerned for the safety of his daughter.

Geff had a habit of throwing things, heavy things, that would go flying through the air. And he displayed a fondness for throwing things in Voirrey's room in particular. Mr. Irving had felt it necessary to remove his daughter from her bedroom and move her into the bedroom he shared with his wife. Once tucked into bed with her parents, a powerful force on the other side of the door bent the door inwards, causing it to bulge wildly as if it would give and break. Then came Geff's high-pitched voice; 'I'm coming in!'

Said the Peel City Guardian; 'Many who have listened, have, at the sound of his voice, felt the hair rising and the spine shivering – sure signs of the presence of the unnatural.'

Mr Irving tried to kill Geff with a gun – but this of course had not been effective, because he could not see Geff. Geff's response to the gun had been to unleash ungodly screams that nearly shattered the family's eardrums, so affronted was Geff by this threat of violence to him. Geff retaliated with his words too, threating imminent violence to the family if Mr Irving did not cease. In fact, it was some weeks before hostilities ceased and Geff stopped issuing the family with threats.

Geff threatened more than just the family on occasions. Charles Morrison, a life-long pal of the father, described the time he heard Geff shouting; "Tell Arthur Morrison (Charles's father) not to come. I won't speak if he does come. I'll blow his brains out." This was followed by the sounds of heaving, pounding and thumping from behind the wood panelling, and the pounding was coming from more than one place – it was coming from all corners of the house, at the same time.

He told the family once; "I am not evil. I could be if I wanted to be. You don't know what damage or harm I could do if I were roused. I could kill you all."

A Captain M. H. Macdonald, who was a businessman and a racing car driver, visited the farm on several occasions. One day, he and Mr. Irving walked a distance of four miles to the village of Peel where they had lunch and a pint of beer. They chatted idly on their walk and for some reason the topic of Mrs. Irving's shoes came up.

When they returned home later to the farm, Mrs. Irving greeted them at the front door and was able to describe their exact conversation on the topic of her shoes – because Geff had already told her. The men agreed, she had recalled what they said most precisely. The captain was also treated to a game of 'heads or tails' with Geff, who tossed the coin through an opening of the wooden panels.

In one incident, a gang of workmen carrying out road repairs watched in astonishment as a piece of bread one of them had thrown away into the field, appeared to be moving on its own across the field. On another occasion, a cousin of Mr Irving was tilling in a field when he felt stones being thrown at him – yet he could see no perpetrator.

Geff grew fond of Voirrey though, and it was said that he would follow the wild child out onto the moors and throw stones at anyone she met on her walks. He guarded her jealously and it was said that he had a remarkably accurate aim when he hit people with the stones. Soon, hundreds of rabbits would begin to be found, their bodies lying strewn across the moors and fields. Geff said he did this so that the family could eat the rabbits or sell them to other islanders for profit. His preferred method of killing was to strangle the rabbits!

In time, Geff told the Irving's that he had come from India, where he said he had often been shot at by farmers. He said that he had lived with a man who wore a green turban on his head. He explained that he had then travelled with a man named 'Holland' from India onto Egypt, and then from Egypt he had arrived in England.

He declared that he had been born in 1852 on June 7th. This would make him 83 years of age. He also said that he came from "the fifth dimension." On another occasion he said, "I am the Holy Ghost." At other times, he declared himself an ordinary ghost and threatened; "I will haunt you with clanking chains."

As the months passed, his mischievous behaviour continued. He bit Mrs Irving's finger when she pocked it though the wood panels. He would regularly lock the daughter in her room from the outside. He would laugh raucously whenever he found out any new gossip to tell them, or when the gossip was later revealed to be true.

He would hurl their furniture across rooms just for the fun of it. He seemed to have the power of telekinesis – able to make objects move of their own accord. He also began to show himself, just occasionally, to the family.

At first, he told them; "I might let you see me some time, but thou wilt never get to know what I am!" His first appearance seemed to be accidental, and happened when the daughter, Voirrey, hid outside and caught a fleeting glimpse of him.

Then he showed himself standing in the rafters of the ceiling. In fact, he even allowed them to photograph him once – although he declared himself to be very nervous, and they found he could not stand still. The black and white photographs came out too blurry.

For those who were granted the privilege of seeing him, they described his appearance as a bit like a squirrel, with a long bushy tail and light brown fur, small ears and a "pushed-in face." His little front paws were described as "hand-like" with 3 fingers and a thumb. No mammal yet discovered has 3 fingers and a thumb though. He was also described as appearing like a cat, or a pig's head.

News of Geff's strange existence at the farm reached mainland England and the newspapers sent reporters to the tiny island. A reporter for the Manchester Daily Dispatch wrote that they heard Geff talk to them. A newspaper from the United States even offered Geff a sum of $50,000 to come and tour the country. (This was a huge sum of money in those days.)

Famed British paranormal investigator Harry Price took a journey to the island to investigate. He brought with him a reporter, Mr. R.S. Lambert of the B.B.C. Lambert would later win libel damages in a courtroom from accusers who declared there was no truth to this mysterious creature and that Lambert was 'deranged.' The court for its part, took the view that Lambert's investigation of Geff was not a sign of madness, and he was awarded him the substantial sum of £7500 in damages. The case was even discussed in the House of Lords.

Sadly, for Lambert and Price however, when they were given a fur sample said to have come from Geff, it did disappoint them when it turned out, according to the Zoological Society who analysed it, to be most likely sheep dog hair. Photos taken by the Society for Psychical Research were unable to prove his existence too – their quality varied and were indistinct. On the other hand, the

Irving's told investigators, and apparently Geff himself said, that he did not want to show himself to investigators for fear they would capture him and take him away for examination.

In a 1932 interview with the Manchester Daily Dispatch, Mr James described Geff as "a little animal resembling a stoat, ferret, or weasel." How could a weasel throw furniture across a room, make a door bulge as though it were about to break, and strangle hundreds of rabbits with its 'hands'? And speak in multiple languages? Yet the investigators spoke to many witnesses, all who testified that this was no hoax, and they themselves felt convinced that this was something so out of the ordinary as to be wholly inexplicable. They wondered though, could Geff be the result of a bizarre Folie à Deux, a mass delusion among the trio living there?

All the reporters and investigators were disappointed that Geff never showed himself to them, but Geff delcared, "They would put me in a bottle!" Another esteemed investigator, Dr Nandor Fodor of the Society for Psychical Research, a trained psychoanalyst, also became convinced that Geff was indeed genuine. Fodor considered the idea of Geff as akin to a witches' familiar.

Geff grew shy of being around when the reporters or investigators came. As soon as they'd gone however, he would return to his fun again. Though he was closer to the family now, and they seemed to tolerate his cohabitation without the ongoing threats from him, he would still hurl insults at them when he felt like it. One time, when Mr Irving was reading his newspaper quietly, Geff shouted; "Read it out, you fat-headed gnome!" Geff said he did this, "for devilment!" The Isle of Man newspapers called him 'The Spook of Dalby," or 'The Buggane."

Over half a century after Geff's occupation of the remote and isolated farmhouse, Voirrey, the daughter, maintains this was no hoax. She wished that it were, for all the disadvantageous publicity it attracted into her family's life, but she is adamant that Geff existed. Interviewed by Fate magazine in the 1970's, she told them she was labelled as being "mental" and her life made a misery because of it.

Of Geff, she said, "His voice was very high-pitched. He swore a lot. At first, he talked to me more than anyone. We carried on regular conversations. It was not a hoax.

But I do wish he had left us alone. I wish it had never happened. I had to leave the Isle of Man. We were snubbed. The other children used to call me "The Spook." Gef has even kept me from getting married," she says.

For those who say it was a clever hoax and the daughter must have been a talented ventriloquist performing 'parlour tricks,' it seems that many witnesses said they heard the voice of Geff when she was no - where near the house. In fact, 18 people signed statements, according to the Isle of Man Examiner, that they had witnessed unaccountably strange things happen in the house.

The voice of Geff would often sound as though it was coming from different parts of the house at the same time. How did Geff do that? How did he know island gossip before the family did? And how did he literally strangle hundreds of rabbits…?

# Chapter Five:

# Taken by the Fey

Readers of my earlier books may recall the strange story of Netta Fornario, and it was one of the first stories of unexplained mystery that I came across, and it has beguiled me ever since. Did the spirit of a dead woman come back to kill Netta? Or, was she killed by the Immortal race of the Fairies?

It's a gothic, Victorian tale of magic and mystery, murder and madness, and the yearning for immortality. It is ripe for a chapter in a Penny Dreadful; but this is a true story. It is a tale that grips as it horrifies; fascinates yet simultaneously strikes at the fear inside of us all, that if we were to delve into the supernatural, it may show us where its allegiances lie, and destroy us entirely.

The location of this tale is the tiny ancient island of Iona, an Island in the Outer Hebredies off the Coast of Scotland. It is 1929, and a young woman has gone missing. When she is found, she is naked and dead and lying on a cross cut into the earth on top of a 'faerie mound.' There is a knife in her hand and a look of terror etched across her face. She has no wounds. She is barefoot but the soles of her feet are clean. Her story encompasses the most cryptic unsolved disappearance and death of an eccentric student of the esoteric arts, whose adventures into 'the Nether World,' would appear to be her undoing.

Iona is a mystical place, rich in the lore of dragons, angels, and vengeful faeries. Its victim is perhaps a naive adept of the occult, who believed she could step into 'Summerland,' the astral plane of Heaven, and return unscathed. One of her best friends, Dion Fortune said, "I do not object to reasonable risks, but it appeared to me that 'Mac' as we called her, was going into very deep waters ... and there was certain to be trouble sooner or later."

In the early 1900's, Marie Nora Emily Edith Fornario, most commonly known as Netta, spent much of her early life in the affluent London suburb of Kew. From a young age she'd shown a keen interest in the rising field of spiritualism and the possibility of communing with the dead, and perhaps this had arisen from the loss of her Mother. She was not close to her father, a doctor who had remarried and was now living in Egypt.

Those who knew her said she had an extraordinary intelligence, and as a young woman she wrote articles for The Occult Review. She preferred solitude, and rarely socialized except for attending Spiritualist meetings and Psychic gatherings. She joined the Alpha and Omega Temple. This had been established in 1888 as an off-shoot of the infamous Hermetic Order of the Golden Dawn, and the Temple was established by ritual magician Samuel Liddell Mathers after his expulsion from the Golden Dawn.

Mathers was a prominent occult scholar who had led a revivalist movement of the esoteric and occult in the late 1800's. He had held office in the Rosicrucian's before founding The Golden Dawn, where he created ritual occult workings by studying the ancient Egyptian magick systems and Dr John Dee's Enochian magick, to create a potent array of rituals.

Sir Arthur Conan Doyle was one of the many prominent members there, as was Irish poet William Butler Yeats. 'Dracula' author Bram Stoker was alleged to be a member, and 'The Beast,' also known as 'The Wickedest Man in the World' Aleister Crowley, was initiated into the Order at the age of 23, shortly after leaving Cambridge University. However, a battle of ego and magickal power ensued between the founder Matthers, and Crowley.

Fighting for control of the Order, it's said that the pair engaged in a fierce battle of spiritual warfare, with Mathers summoning a vampire entity to attack Crowley, while Crowley retaliated by unleashing Beelzebub and an army of 49 demons against Mathers, after his beloved bloodhounds suddenly died, at the hands of this vampire Crowley believed. When Mathers died some years later, no cause of death was given, and while his wife Mona said he had contracted Spanish influenza, privately she was said to have been most concerned that Crowley had claimed the life of his arch-nemesis through spiritual attack, and she too now feared retaliation from this potent magician, it was said. This would become relevant to the fate of Netta.

Both Mathers and Crowley ended up being expelled from the Golden Dawn as a result of their shenanigans, and Mathers then founded his own order, The Alpha and Omega Temple. Thirty years later, Miss Netta Fornario came along and joined them. This occult Order included the wife of author Oscar Wilde, and it drew on a synthesis of Western magick tradition including kabbalah, alchemy, divination, astrology, masonic symbolism and ritual magick, adapting systems of magick from ancient Egypt and England's Dr. John Dee. Dee was perhaps the most famous hermetician and he happened to have lived in Mortlake, near Kew, where Netta now lived. Sometimes referred to as 'The Queen's Conjuror,' for his alleged influence on Queen Elizabeth I, and indeed he is also known as the original 007, Dr. Dee lived at Mortlake from 1565 to 1595. He created Enochian Magick, based on 'the language of Angels.' His assistant, Edward Kelly, would stare at a flat 'shew' stone, or mirror, and believed he was in direct communication with angels. Dr. Dee would write down the messages the angels gave, in this 'Enochian language of Spells,' which became widely used by practitioners of the occult ever since the 1600's. Unfortunately, the majority of Dr. Dee's writings were destroyed by fire at his home and the few that survived are now housed in the British museum, but he was perhaps the most influential magician ever known and he may well have been one of the reasons Netta set out on her left-hand path.

Netta was raised by her maternal grandparents in Mortlake, Kew, after the loss of her mother shortly after her birth. She was raised in a strictly protestant household, but as she grew to adulthood, Netta quickly found herself turning to spiritualism to meet her need for esoteric knowledge and perhaps for desired contact with her deceased mother. She was a regular attendee at meetings of the Alpha et Omega Temple, and she developed close friendships there.

This really was at the height of the Spiritualist movement in Victorian England. Sir Arthur Conan Doyle in 1918, wrote that this movement 'Is infinitely nearer to positive proof (of the after-life) than any other religious development with which I am acquainted.' Leading cultural figures were immersing themselves in a quest for transcendence, life after death, and sacred knowledge through this pursuit of spiritualism. For Netta however, her keen interest soon turned to obsession. She believed she could heal people through 'Telepathy,' and would often spend great amounts of time attempting to do so. As she reached the age of 33, she decided to set off for an extended stay on the tiny and remote island of Iona in the Hebrides, off the West coast of Scotland. At the time, houses on the Island had no electricity, no heating, no running water, and there were no phones or daily newspapers, but it was an ancient place renown for peace and tranquillity. Perhaps Netta sought the solitude it offered, and it could be a place for reflection and calm; but there was a lot more to Iona than that.

Legendary English Diarist Dr Samuel Johnson wrote of his visit to Iona, describing the strange magnetic energy of the Island and its powerful effect on him. Pre-Raphaelite artist John Duncan would go to Iona to paint, and he spoke of hearing 'faiery music' in the distance while he worked. He also told of his many encounters with the Faiery race.

In the 7th century, Abbot of Iona, a monk named Adomnán, wrote in his journals about Saint Columba, who legend had it could control the weather on the Island and keep the dragons at bay. The Abbot wrote of encounters with such creatures, as well as his own visitations by Angelic beings.

Perhaps that is why this mystical retreat now became home to Netta, for it was known by those closest to her that she had become fixated with the need to communicate with the supernatural and the dead, through any means.

On her arrival at Iona, she found lodgings with a family there. The Scotsman of 27th November 1929, writes 'This "alien" woman, who dressed in the fashion of the Arts and Crafts movement – with long cape and hand-woven tunic – settled into the house of someone only known as Mrs MacRae. The 33-year-old Fornario spent her time walking the island and in long trances.' She was a bohemian, with alluring dark eyes and long black hair, always worn in braids. She wore long robes, and would have been viewed as arty, eccentric, or in modern times as a hippie or 'new-ager.'

It was later reported that she spent almost all her time alone in her bedroom, or out on the moors at night. It seemed that she would spend almost all of her nights out roaming alone then returning in the early mornings to write in a journal in her room.

As an initiate of an esoteric order, Netta was a practicing occult adept and she was of the belief that one of her callings was to heal people, through telepathy. In fact, prior to her death, she'd sent a message to her housekeeper in Kew, saying not to expect her back from Iona anytime soon, because she was presently engaged in 'a terrible case of healing going on.' We do not know who she was attempting to heal, but it was also said that she appeared to wanted to 'heal' the Island too. Dedemia Harding of Bradford Golden Dawn says, 'She wanted to bring all the unseen forces at numerous astral levels together in one place which would have created the power for an enormous healing ritual.' It was later believed she had been trying to contact the spirits of the Island, through induced states of trance. She had a habit of falling into extended trances, for hours at a time, and in fact she once told her host on Iona that on one occasion her trance had lasted an entire week; but she had advised her host Mrs. Cameron that should this happen, under no circumstances must a doctor be called. Netta informed her that no medical intervention would be necessary.

Though her father was a doctor, Netta was estranged from him and she had little time for orthodox medicine. Her housekeeper in London, Mrs Veylater said that it was common for her mistress to 'moan and cry out piteously' if she were prevented from healing a person whom she thought she could cure.

No-one really knew exactly what it was Netta did at night when she went out on the moors, but her behaviour was beginning to disturb the family she lodged with. They noticed that her fingernails and jewellery had turned black, and her once healthy skin had grown increasingly pallid. They also said it was almost as though she would look at them with a far-away stare through glazed eyes, not really focused at all on where she was or what they were saying to her.

According to Francis King's 'Ritual Magic in England,' Netta reportedly revealed to Mrs Cameron that "Certain people" were affecting her telepathically and that she was under attack. Then one day she became suddenly terribly distressed. Frantically, she told her host family that she must leave the Island immediately. She would give no reason, and yet the family did not think there was any kind of emergency at her grandparents' home in London, as she had received no telegram.

Her continued insistence that she must leave however, and her increasing state of desperation, led the mother to help her pack up her belongings and the family helped take them down to the harbour, even though they knew that, being Sunday, there were no ferries until the following day.

With her belongings now at the harbour, Netta had no choice but to return to her lodgings, and she remained in her room quietly all day until evening came. She then hurriedly came out of it, telling the surprised family that she no longer needed to leave. They would later describe, that as she said this, her face bore the expression of resignation. That she spoke as though there was some kind of fatalistic inevitability; as though her destiny were sealed, and there was no way to change things now.

It was later reported in The Scotsman that when she informed her host she must return to London, she had spoken of a rudderless boat that went across the sky, and she talked of messages she had received from 'Other Worlds.'

The following day, the Mother of the family, Mrs. Cameron, realized that she had not seen or heard Netta all day, which was unusual, because Netta's habit was to go out at night and then spend the day in her room. Mrs. Cameron had heard no sounds of movement at all. A little puzzled, she knocked on Netta's door several times, but on receiving no replies, she opened the door to find the room empty, although several of Netta's personal belongings were still there. Curiously, in the bedroom fireplace lay the burnt embers of what looked like a manuscript. Her bed appeared not to have been slept in.

Very concerned now, after Netta's recent unexplained distress, the mother, father and son decided to set out across the moors of the tiny 3.5 x 1-mile Island to look for her. They searched for hours, but they found no sign of her in the wilderness. That night, Netta did not return home.

The next morning, the family arranged for one of the Islanders to go to the Mainland and bring back a policeman. When the policeman duly arrived, he, accompanied by many volunteers who lived on the Island, set out again in search of her. They covered the Island from end to end, width to width. It was late in the evening that the son of the family she lodged with stumbled across a horrifying sight. He had been led to the scene by the barking of a dog, and the dog had taken the boy right to the spot where Netta's dead body now lay. It was an isolated spot of peat bogs on a 'faiery mound' on the south of Loch Staonaig. Netta was lying on the cold ground, naked apart from a long black robe which had some kind of sigils on the lapel. The ground beneath her body appeared to have been carved into the shape of a large cross. In her left hand she held a long knife, which had to be pried out of her death-grip. Her face was said to have been fixed into a death-mask expression of pure terror. Her body was lined with fierce, deep scratch marks, according to the report of her best friend, Dion Fortune.

The cross shape beneath her body was speculated to have been carved by her, and it was suggested that this could perhaps have been done by Netta, as some form of attempt to defend herself from some kind of attack, or perhaps as part of some kind of magick ritual she might have been carrying out.

The very strange thing that stood out to the policeman was that her toes were cut and bruised and this seemed to indicate that she had been running at speed over rocks and rough ground, as though she was being chased; as though she had been running for her life, and yet the soles of her feet were in no way damaged or injured. How was this possible? How had she travelled over rough, broken and sometimes perilous terrain without sustaining any injuries to the soles of her feet? How were her feet entirely clean, untouched and unmarked?

What also puzzled the policeman and the Islanders too, was how could her body have remained undiscovered for two days, despite the island being a tiny size and the sheer number of thorough searches that had been carried out looking for her? She seemed to have been missing from sight for two days. How could they all have missed her, they all wondered? Her death was determined to have occurred between 10 pm on 17th and 1.30 pm on 19th. Her cause of death was determined to be 'Heart Failure' from exposure; though many believed that from the expression on her face, she must have died of fright, and that terror had taken her life that night. It appeared that Netta may have spent the last few hours of her life in a desperate flight from someone or something. Unusually, for someone suffering 'exposure,' she was not curled up into a ball nor had she tried to burrow in an attempt to keep warm or find shelter, which would have been the usual thing a person would do when suffering from hypothermia, as paradoxical undressing often takes place, which sees the person shedding their clothes in the belief that they are very hot when in fact really it is the cold affecting their nerves. If Netta had left her lodgings dressed in more than a black cloak, then where were her clothes now? Had she worn no underwear? Although of course, magick rituals do often require nudity, so perhaps that is how she had gone out. No clothes were found beside her, nor anywhere else on the small island.

There were whispered rumors from some Islanders of the sighting of a mysterious cloaked figure being seen with Netta shortly before her disappearance, and there were also reports of strange glowing blue lights in the sky, which no-one could explain.

After Netta was found spread-eagled and dead on the faery mound with her face fixed in the rigor of absolute horror, The Scotsman wrote, 'Whether she died from a mystic dual, was killed by a feuding member of an occult organisation, or simply died from exposure ... there is no doubt that the story leaves some unanswered questions.'

Dion Fortune declared, on hearing of the terrible and strange death of her good friend Netta, that Moina Mathers, the wife of their leader of the Alpha et Omega Temple, had killed Netta. This was strange, because Moina herself was dead too. Fortune declared that Moina had done this by means of 'astral assassination.' Moina Mathers was known as the "seeress" of the Temple, and she was said to have provided a great amount of occult 'information' to the Order through her mediumship abilities. She was also a talented artist. She met Samuel Liddell Mathers, their leader, at the British Museum. After his death in 1918, she became head of a successor organization calling itself the Rosicrucian Order of the Alpha et Omega. When her husband had died, Moina had become convinced that her husband's death had been caused by a combination of exhaustion brought on by incessant communication from his "Secret Chiefs"; supernatural beings who channelled occult information to him, and, through psychic astral attack by his old enemy Aleister Crowley. Indeed, Moina herself expressed fear that Crowley would come after her as his next victim. In the new Order she had established, Monia was assisted by a mysterious unnamed man called 'Frater X.' Dione

Fortune's assertion was that Moina practised Black Magic and Fortune was firmly of the opinion that Moina was responsible for Netta's death on Iona, despite Moina being long-since dead. According to Radina Pitt though, when Dion Fortune was still a member of the Alpha and Omega, Moina had accused Fortune of revealing secrets of the Order in her writings. It was said that this was the reason why Moina expelled Fortune from the order. Could this have caused Fortune to cast a finger of guilt at Moina, without warrant? Or, was there truth to her accusation? And just how do you kill someone when you yourself are dead, using astral assassination?

Dion Fortune was actually the pseudonym of Violet Mary Firth Evans and she was actually not only an esoteric practitioner, but a psychiatrist too. Some say that behind the shadows of Gerald B. Gardner, England's foremost Witch, lurked Dion Fortune. Her mentor had been the head of the Theosophical society, Dr. Theodore Moriarty, (who sounds like he belongs in a Sherlock Holmes book). He was an occultist and a freemason. He set up a co-masonic lodge in Hammersmith London, with unusually mostly if not all female 'officers,' including Netta Fornario, who held the position of 'Outer Guardian' officer.

Had powerful dark forces been sent to kill Netta? Or had she herself taken a step too far into the shadowy realms of the astral worlds and naively unleashed demonic forces that had dragged her to hell itself? At least four of Aleister Crowley's known mistresses were found dead, all allegedly killing themselves in quick succession; or, were they too killed by some form of attack, by forces summoned in dark rituals? As for Netta's pursuits and her subsequent strange demise, her friend Dion Fortune offered, "At one time, we did work together, but before her death we went our separate ways. I don't object to reasonable risk, but it appeared she was going in too deep, and trouble would come. Whether she was killed by psychic attack, stayed out on the astral plane too long, or whether she strayed into an elemental kingdom who shall know? The facts however cannot be questioned.'

Head of the Order, Samuel Mathers himself claimed to be able to summon the demon Beelzebub, but he had given very strict and ominous warnings to fellow members of the Order that unless the magical circle of protection was created with pristine accuracy, the magician would be killed instantly or would self-destruct as a result of perilously imprecise summoning during these treacherous ritual workings.

Said Fortune, "She was especially interested in the Green Ray elemental contacts; too much interested in them for my peace of mind, and I became nervous and refused to cooperate with her."

Who are The Green Ray elementals? They are said to derive from 'the Seven Rays,' in esoteric philosophies such as Theosophy and Gnosticism. The 'Rays' are types of light-matter, comprised of waves and energy that are thought to have created the Universe.

'The Green Ray' is believed to be on a stratum of the etheric planes, located at a higher level than those of the lower astral planes where the darker demons and deities of Babylon and Akkad dwell. The 'Green Ray' is thought to be the etheric plane where the Fey race; the faeries, and other Nature Spirits dwell. Netta was trying to gain entry to this plane of energy and vibration in which the Faeries are said to live; but did she erringly enter the lower planes instead, where demons and darkness claim dominion?

Or, did the Faeries themselves turn against her, and hurl their wrath upon her? Although 'The Fey' are historically known to refer to themselves as 'The Gentry,' Scholars versed in their lore would be quick to point out that the Faiery race are nature spirits whose loyalty does not lie with humans.

When Netta lived in London, she had been obsessed by the writings of Fiona MacLeod, or rather, the writer William Sharp, a Scottish poet and novelist who also wrote under the pen-name of Fiona MacLeod. At one point, Netta had gone to see an Opera that was based on MacLeod's writing, more than twenty times, and she wrote a subsequent review of the production.

The Opera was a tale of Faerie folk and magic, in which the Fey are cast as a breed of strong immortals that humans are in fear yet awe of, because of their supreme ability to interfere with and manipulate humans. Netta, it seems, had an unwavering fascination with the Faiery race. She wrote of 'Students of mysticism who are able to understand the great truths behind the gossamer curtain of the Fey,' presumably classing herself as one of these students.

However, she also mentions the appearance of the demonic in the Opera, 'Symbolising dark atavism,' and crucially she points out, 'The reaction of these 'lower principles' to the stimulus of super consciousness often produces disastrous results.'

In other words, supernatural entities may react strongly to anyone who attempted to reach and interact with their hidden realms; thus implying that she did seem well aware of the dangers of attempting to enter the unseen world, and of the very strong possibility of being confronted with the malignant forces that dwelt within it.

This knowledge however did not stop her quest. In her review of McLeod's opera, published in the Occult Review, she quotes the lines of a character from the original written version, "There is no dream save the dream of death," and she interprets this line as explicitly meaning that 'death itself is only a dream; the ultimate reality lies in the other world where all of life is one,' as MacLeod wrote. Netta remonstrates that these lines were left out of the Opera and they should not have been. This perhaps is a crucial clue that Netta wished to go there – to the land beyond death, where life for her was more real; so that after bodily death, she could continue in a land where time never ended.

Why did she go to the Island of Iona? Well, her favourite author, McLeod, had a very strong connection to the Island. He had spent his childhood there. As William Sharpe, he had written 'Hebridean Legends,' and curiously, in his book he tells the story of an incident that happened when he was a boy.

One day, he went to call on his friend Elsie, who he hadn't seen for a few days. When he got to her house, her Mother was there but Elsie wasn't, and he asked her mother where she was. Her mother answered cryptically that Elsie had been gone for a few days now. Sharpe wondered how he could not have known this, as the Island was so tiny everyone knew everybody's business. Elsie's mother said that as Elsie left, 'She turned an' smiled an' because o' that terrifying smile I couldna say a word.' Elsie's mother continued, telling him that her daughter had believed she was in communication with the long-dead spirits of the monks who had once lived on the Island. She said that her daughter believed the monks were attacking her and that she must go to the only place on the Island where she would be safe; a place where they would not be able to follow her - to the Faiery mound. Where Netta was later to be found dead.

Elsie's mother went on to tell him of how, long ago, when the Monks had lived in a commune on the Island, "They burnt a woman. She wasn't a woman - but they thought she was. She was a Faerie; a 'Sheen.' And it's ill to any that bring harm to them." Elsie's mother said that though the spirits of the dead monks were still very strong, they were not able to enter Faiery land; a particular spot on the Island along a path which led to a Faiery mound, and this was where her daughter had gone to seek refuge.

It was at this exact spot that Netta's body had been found. What exactly happened to Netta, has never really been solved. There was no autopsy and she was buried within days. The place where she was found is well known to the Island folk. It is called the 'Faery Mound,' or 'Druid's Hill'. It has long been associated with magic and superstition and supernatural visitations.

During her stay on Iona, Netta's host family were alarmed that all her Silver Jewellery had turned black, along with her fingernails. A humid climate can cause this, but Iona is far from humid. An acidic body also can be the cause, but so too can supernatural visitations. For aeons, tales of encounters with demons, aliens, fairies, and all manner of undefined entities have been described as arriving with the most overpowering stench of sulphur. Sulphur turns silver black too. Is this the most compelling evidence that she had gone too far into the realm of the land of the Fey? Had the powerful breed of fairy folk killed her?

Author Richard Wilson tracked down the son of the family she lodged with in 1929, Callum Cameron, who was 12 years old when Netta stayed with them. He said that when she died on 'Sithean Mor,' the faery mound, "Netta was digging in the ground - She was digging to try to get to the Faeries inside." Had her soul been taken inside the faery mound and the shell of her body left behind? After Netta's death, her housekeeper in London told the Newspapers, "Several times she had been to the far beyond and had come back to life after spending some time in another world." This time however, Netta did not come back.

But how did she get to the spot in which she was found, in bare feet, yet with the soles of her feet uninjured and completely unmarked? 'The only injuries are to the upper part of her toes,' writes the Scottish Correspondent, 'which are torn and bloody. The sole explanation is that she has been running on her toes. It is well known that witches can travel long distances by skimming along the ground on the front of their toes, creating an appearance of floating. For the Islanders this is conclusive proof she is a witch. There is no sign she has been dragged there.' Another rather outlandish theory was also put forward by Ron Haliday, a paranormal researcher who said it was entirely possible that this was because she had been levitating at the time, while writer Alastair Alpin Macgregor suggests she was in a trance. 'Netta had told people she went to Iona as she had 'the call of the island,' but he questions the circumstances surrounding what lead to her death. 'How otherwise (than in a trance) could a woman unable in the ordinary way to proceed on foot more than a few hundred yards at a time, have travelled so far over territory so precipitous, so broken, so perilous? Whereas her heels and much of the soles of her feet were in no way injured, her toes were torn and bleeding. She must have reached that hollow of death by hurrying through the heather and over the rocks on the tips of her toes.'

Why was she fleeing so desperately? It was as though she had been fleeing on tip-toes, her toes all torn-up and bloodied, and run she may have, for the death-mask of terror seems to imply this had to be the case. Yet how could the soles of her feet be so clean and uninjured?

Despite her fragile health on that fateful night, must we presume she fled someone or something; like the Vampire, summoned to attack Aleister Crowley by Samuel Matthers? Or the legion of demons, sent in retaliation by Crowley? Dion fortune, when describing the sharp deep scratches found on Netta's body; (although it is not revealed how she knew this) adds that she had knowledge of other victims of psychic attack who also, just like Netta, had been found with strange scratch marks on their bodies. She also revealed that she herself had experienced an astral attack upon herself that left her with 'shattered health.'

"I know for myself the peculiar horror of such an experience; its insidiousness, its potency, and its disastrous effects on mind and body," she says, adding, "It is not easy to get people to come forward and bear witness… they know there is very little likelihood of their being believed, and they will be more likely to earn themselves a reputation for mental unbalance than for anything else. Secondly, because any tampering with the foundations of the personality is an experience of such peculiar and unique horror that the mind shrinks from the contemplation of it, one cannot talk about it.'

Was a preternatural creature hunting Netty that night? Had Moina Matthers summoned and commanded a beast from the underworld to do her bidding and attack Netta?

Or, was there a more human hand at play here? How did Netta manage to get so far in bare feet and in poor health? Could someone have carried her? Dion Fortune said, 'She had evidently been on an astral expedition from which she never returned,' but added, 'She was a not a good subject for such experiments, for she suffered from some defect of the pituitary body.' It seems that some reports say she stayed in her room quite a lot due to weakness in her physical condition. Burning the candle at night, she wore herself out with incessant writing in her journal until dawn. It was said that though she roamed wildly alone at night across the heather moors and beaches, she was also accordingly unable to walk too far in one go, and frequently had to stop to rest. Says Mary Irvine for the

Scottish Correspondent, 'Netta is not in good health. Daily exercise is a few hundred yards walk along the beach, close to her lodgings. Some days she is so tired she does not leave her room.' She was a mile away from the farmhouse when she was found; which is quite some distance for someone described as being in poor health.

What about the rumour of a cloaked figure seen with Netta on the night she disappeared? Was this just gossip and speculation, or had another figure stalked her from London to the sacred Isle? The Sinister Path is the name given to those who pursue dark occultism, and so had her foe actually been of the human kind? How did her body go unnoticed for two days on this tiny open island? Had she been pursued, held somewhere and then killed in a hideous open-air sacrifice, as revenge of some kind? Wrote the Occult review in February 1930, 'One newspaper alludes to 'Mysterious stories on the island, about blue lights having been seen in the vicinity of where her body was found, and there is also a story of a cloaked man.'

Could poison – a deadly plant or herb have rendered Netta unconscious and incapable, and her killer left her to die of the cold on a freezing moor? Or was it magic powers?

Dedemia Harding of the Bradford Golden Dawn says, 'Netta is said to have offended Moina Mathers, wife of Samuel Mathers and one of the founders of the Golden Dawn.' She also adds, 'Being born in Cairo, she was perhaps already closer to the Mysteries (Mystery schools) than those who tried to emulate the Egyptian magic with the Golden Dawn, as Netta was a true Egyptian; something her occult temple contemporaries could only dream of, and something that may have caused bad feeling amongst them. We only have the islanders accounts of what happened, which could conceivably be at best misleading. Netta was buried under equally mysterious circumstances. Why no proper autopsy was ever done further fuels the mystery.' Says Wilson, 'The alleged penalty for breaking this group's oath of silence was to be subjected to a 'current of will, which,' he says, 'would cause the offender to become "paralysed as if blasted by lightning or fall dead."'

Yet, was the biggest foe inside Netta's own mind? When author Richard Wilson tracked down the son of the family Netta had lodged with, Callum Cameron, he said it was just a normal kitchen knife, and no cross was carved in the turf. The boy's opinion of Netta was that she was just weird. "She was a disturbed woman, that's all." In this former 12-year-old boy's mind, she was an eccentric, and her undoing was misadventure – she died of exposure, he said, just like the Doctor determined. Was he earnest, as we must assume, or could he be playing down the oddities of the case? Was Netta possibly the victim of some sort of magic attack, or, had she driven herself mad? Did she develop schizophrenia, and believed she was being attacked, when in reality, this was all in her mind?

Aleister Crowley's first wife Rose died in a lunatic asylum. His second wife went insane. The most commonly quoted excerpt regarding Crowley's romantic relationships is, 'Five mistresses committed suicide, and scores ended in the gutter as alcoholics, drug addicts or in mental institutions.' There is another story which perhaps could bear some resemblance to the fate of Netta. It took place in another very ancient and mystical place, in Cornwall, in the South West of England in the year 1938, and it led to a most unexpected death of another woman after the ritual summoning of the Devil himself, apparently, in a cottage rented by Aleister Crowley. The lady was a Mrs. Katherine Laird Arnold-Forster, and she either died of a stroke, or the other version says the Devil took her as his own, after frightening her to death. Her companion, Gerald Vaughan, who had been present that evening, became mad and had to be taken to a lunatic asylum to live out the rest of his life in insanity.

Netta was delving into the unknown, risking the fracture of her mind by seeking contact with immortals and elementals, and roaming alone into the night in solitude, with just her own thoughts. This surely could be sufficient to drive a person insane, notwithstanding any faeries, spirits or demons? In other words, was her persecution all in her mind?

She believed that she could see the faces of previous patients of hers in the clouds. She spoke of rudderless boats that crossed the sky. She thought she could heal people – without even touching them and with no medical training whatsoever. Her housekeeper in London said she once embarked on a 40-day fast, although fortunately she gave in shortly after, the housekeeper added. In London, she became transfixed and so obsessed by an Opera about the Immortal Faieries that she went to see it 23 times. Had her strenuous pursuits toward supernatural powers affected her health and mind so badly, mainly through self-neglect of her body, and we could say of her mind, that she had driven herself into lunacy, and the demons and the Fairies were merely of her own mind? Although, her story is very like the fate of Elsie, who herself vanished on the Faery mound.

We still do not know how she got to the spot in which she died, barefoot, with clean feet. How could she have travelled over rough land with no marks on her feet? Was there some kind of involvement among the Islander's themselves? Had she been borne to the spot at which she was to die?

Could someone else have carved the cross into the earth; someone offended by this 'witch' and her non-Christian activities, on an island considered to be the seat of Christianity? Did an islander kill her, in a rite of sacrifice, like the ghastly film 'The Wicker Man?' Was she offered up as a human sacrifice, like St Columba's beloved friend Anadnon, as an offering to the gods who protected Iona? Iona was firmly a Christian abode. Formed from rock so ancient it is believed by many to be one of the most sacred places on earth. Victorian writer and Netta's idol, Fiona Macleod, poetically expressed: "To tell the story of Iona is to go back to God, and to end in God." According to St Columba's strong beliefs, he felt he must offer a living sacrifice on the Island. He must bury someone alive in the foundations of his chapel, he announced, and a willing victim stepped forward to offer himself; his friend Oran. Oran was as such therefore buried alive in the foundations. As this was taking place, Columba apparently requested that Oran's face be left uncovered so that Columba could say farewell to his beloved friend. It's believed Oran, midway, changed his mind about dying however, and began to shout out and blaspheme, to which Columba decided his face must be covered after all!

Prior to this, the island was held precious by the Druids. Before St Columba settled here, Iona had been known by the old Gaelic name Innis nan Druidhneach; the 'Island of the Druids,' and a primary seat for Pre-Christian Celtic Druid Magi. Scottish researcher Lewis Spence quotes 'Their chief seat in Scotland was the Island of Iona.' Later, in 563 AD, St Columba, the grandson of the Irish king Niall and 12 disciples built a Celtic church on the island and founded a monastic community, and St Columba set about converting Scottish and English pagans to Christianity. Iona became a resting place for kings. A 1549 survey listed '48 Scottish kings and 4 Irish kings' buried there. Columba banished all women from the island, for they were 'mischief.' Did this still ring true now? Were the islanders affronted, insulted, angered, by this woman's pro-occult proclivities, in an established Christian land? She is out at night, wandering naked except for a dark robe, practising strange rites, and the rumours spread? This is heresy! This is the devil's work! And yet, Iona is known as a place long-since attracting more spiritually-minded folk, although Netta was perhaps one of the most eccentric to venture there.

Did they fear this 'witch' at a time when 'new-age' was less wide-spread, less acceptable than in our modern times? Had she no right in treading on their ancient land, disturbing the long-dead, trying to 'heal' the land and contacting the spirits? Was she tampering in a place sacred to them, long-since established by St Columba as a Christian, not Pagan, dwelling-place? Did they come together in secrecy to rid themselves of this dark-eyed occultist?

Or perhaps she frightened someone, who upon seeing her naked with a sharp knife in her hand and a far-off gaze in her eyes, perhaps attacked her in what they believed was a pre-emptive strike of self-defence? And yet, she had no wounds save on her feet, unless we believe what one of her closest friends revealed some years later, that her body bore sinisterly deep scratches.

Bradford New society of the Golden Dawn wrote, 'One psychic envisioned a man in his 30's with a moustache as her killer. We think Fornario was strangled, probably by an Iona islander and the matter hushed up.' Or was she 'silenced' by members of her Order, for an as yet unknown revelation of their secrets? Had an associate disapproved of her, been jealous of her, or felt she had shunned the sacred oath of her brethren in some way by revealing secrets that could only be dealt with by death as punishment?

Was she murdered by a mortal? Or had her adventures with the Green Ray Faeries seen a swift and violent backlash from them; the race who has no empathy or kinship with humans. Was she now in Summerland, the astral plane of Heaven, or had the Faeries taken her soul? In Celtic mythology and theosophy, the 'Realm of the Dead,' or 'Summerland' is the home of the spirits and the

Sidhe; the Sheen, the Faeries. In Netta's review of 'The Immortal Hour' Opera, she emphasised the vital importance of the lines, "There is no dream, save this, the dream of death" implying that death itself is only a dream and that the ultimate reality lies in the 'other world,' Sumerland, where all life is eternal; Her Fairyland. Did the Faeries take her soul and leave her body behind? As the boy of her lodger family said, "Netta was digging in the ground - She was digging to try to get to the Faeries inside."

A number of letters of 'strange character' were said to have been taken by the police, after the discovery of her body, and the police passed them on to the procurator fiscal for consideration. Perhaps they were merely her own journal writing, or maybe they held clues of vital importance? The fate of these letters is not known.

There is a postscript to this story, found in The Scotsman of December 5th in the year of her death. Netta's father is described as being 'seized with great anxiety regarding his daughter. He was unable to account for his fears yet could not shake off the feeling that something was wrong. Two days later a telegram arrived announcing that the dead body of his daughter had just been discovered...' Was she now alive in Sumerland?

## Chapter Six:

## The Ghost Boys

In October 2017, a rare manuscript was discovered in England's North Yorkshire county, detailing a very disturbing 17th century case. The manuscript was discovered when it came up for sale after it had been found by an antiquarian bookseller. It is called 'Demonolgia: A discourse on Witchcraft' and it was written by an Edward Fairfax in the year 1621. He published it after he had failed to get what he believed was a clan of witches, who were making spirits appear to his daughters, convicted in court. The case happened in Fuistone, a small and picturesque valley in the county of Yorkshire.

Mr Fairfax had three daughters, Ann, Elizabeth, and Ellen. His youngest daughter Ann died in October 1621, and he believed a local clan of witches had sent evil spirits that had driven this daughter to her death. In the manuscript, Fairfax describes creatures that he believes to be the witch's familiars, including one of which is 'A deformed thing with many feet, rough with hair... the name of it unknown.'

In the father's diary entry for Wednesday 14th November, he writes, 'She saw a black dog by her bedside,' and, 'She had an apparition of one like a young gentleman, with hat with a gold band.' This spirit gentleman 'told her he came to be her suitor. She asked him what he was; 'he said he was a Prince,' and that 'He would make her a Queen if she went with him.' She refused, and said, "In the name of God, what are you? Come near me and let me feel you." 'He would not do, but said it was no matter for feeling.' "You are the devil and art but a shadow,'" she told him. 'Then he went away, but returned with a fair woman, telling Helen that this woman was far more beautiful than her and he said this was his wife;' but he told Helen he would leave his wife if she, Helen, would go with him. Again, Helen refused to go with him. He left, but returned a little while later. 'He appeared to her again, and this time offered her a knife, moving her to kill herself therewith. She told him she would not. Then he offered her a rope.'

He wanted her to hang herself. But she again refused. 'Then he advised her to take a pin out of her clothes and put it into her mouth.' He was trying to get her to destroy herself. Then, 'He turned into the shape of a beast with many horns. Then was he like a calf. Presently he was like a very little dog, and desired her to open her mouth and let him come into her body, and then he would rule all the world.'

One of the most frightening incidents Fairfax writes about happened on Wednesday the 2nd of January, when his daughter Helen went to the back door of the house after hearing a knock at the door. Upon opening the door, two boys rushed in. 'The little boy caught her about the middle with his hands; the greater held her by the arm with one hand, and with the other stopped her mouth lest she should cry. In great haste they forced her into the back house, told her they had long watched for her, but now they had her and would drown her. She struggled and called to her mother. They said they would soon make her past calling. They brought her to the riverside. One of them said, "This place is not deep enough, let us carry her up-stream." So they did.

'In putting her down, she got hold of the bushes, and she held so fast that the boys could not get her hands loose though they laid hold of her feet and pulled violently. It chanced that Elizabeth Smith, passing by between the barn and the house, espied her holding to the bushes. "Help me Bess, for here is two boys which would put me into the water." Elizabeth Morehouse saw not the boys that took hold of her.' Though Helen was in the midst of being drowned by these two 'boys,' she was the only one who could see them.

We do not know how she finally died, as her father's manuscript breaks off suddenly, but her father firmly believed it was by supernatural figures who attacked her, very possibly it was by these ghost-boys. He was a mathematics professor who taught at university and he took the matter so seriously that he took it to court, blaming local witches who lived near him for setting these ghosts up on his daughter, but the court of course could not prosecute without any solid and tangible evidence at all…

## Chapter Seven:

## Missing: Returned Dead of Fright

On the 6th of June 1980, Zygmunt Adamski disappeared from the village of Todmorden, in the rural county of Yorkshire, after leaving his house on an errand. Five days later, his body was located on the top of a coal pile in a coal supplier's yard. The police attended the scene, and on examination they discovered vivid burn marks on the man's shoulders and neck, and a strange green ointment covering the wounds.

The man's clothes were very clean, despite him having been missing for five days, although the police noticed that his jacket had been buttoned up incorrectly and he did not appear to be wearing a shirt underneath his jacket. Of course, the immediate questions became: how did he die?

And how did he end up on the top of the coal pile? One strange aspect of the man's discovery was that there appeared to be no footsteps leading to the coal pile or in the coal itself, yet he was laying at the top of it. How did he climb up the coal pile without leaving any foot marks in the coal?

The police spoke to the owners of the coal yard. The last person to be in the yard was the coal company's son. He told the police that he had been there in the morning until about midday. He had seen no body on a coal pile then. Mr Adamski's body was transported to the local hospital where a pathologist determined that his death had occurred between eleven and one pm of that day, but that the strange burns on his body had occurred two days before Mr Adamski's death. The coroner, James Turnbull said, "What led to his death couldn't be answered," but he determined that Adamski had died of a heart attack 'due to shock or fright.' His face, at the time of his death, had been contorted in fear. For the pathologist and the police, the circumstances of the man's death were a complete mystery. Quite why Mr Adamski had died, where he had been for several days since he left his house, and what that strange ointment on his wounds was, could not be explained. The case was never solved any further than that. How did he get to the top of that coal pile? What did he see that caused his face to be contorted in fear when he died?

There is an addendum to this unexplained story. Policeman Mr Alan Godfrey had been first to arrive at the scene in the coal yard. A few weeks after this, Mr Godfrey was on a night-shift when something most strange happened. He was out searching for cows that had gone missing from a farmer's field. He could find no sign of them, and he was sitting back in his patrol car when suddenly, a large object appeared in the road ahead of him. It was very big and his first thoughts were that it was a bus that had perhaps broken down. The lights on the object looked strange to him however, and the shape was not that of a bus. He decided to radio for back-up before leaving his vehicle to investigate, but he found that his police radio would not work. Feeling very uneasy, he remained in his car.

Later, he was shocked to discover that nearly an hour of time had passed that he could not account for. Even stranger, the soles of his boots now looked like he had been dragged along the ground. The soles of his shoes were ripped apart. It would later be established that on the same night, other policemen on duty independently called police HQ with alarming reports of seeing strange bright lights in the sky, descending into the valley, and a member of the public who was out driving that night also called the police in concern.

As for the missing cows, they were later discovered in a field which they did not belong in; a field which was locked with a padlocked gate. The ground in the field was very muddy, but oddly, there were no hoof-prints from the cows. How could the cows have entered the field without leaving any prints from their hooves? And how did they enter a locked field? It was almost as though, perhaps like Mr Adamski too, they had been dropped there from above.

Mr Godfrey, the policeman, was so disturbed by all of this that he visited a hypnotherapist who specialised in regression therapy; that is, taking a patient back into a past event. Godfrey was particularly uneasy about the missing time that he could not account for, and under hypnosis, he began to explain that he seemed to find himself in a small room with a black-robed, bearded man who had a "biblical appearance," and who was accompanied by "a huge black dog and other smaller "creatures" that were the size of five-year olds and had robotic movements…"

The ointment found on Mr Adamski's body was never able to be scientifically identified. Why he disappeared only to turn up dead in the most bizarre way, remains an enigmatic mystery.

# Chapter Eight:

# The Hairy Hands

Dartmoor is a beautiful but wild and barren landscape in Devon. Holidaymaker Florence Warwick, 28, was driving along one of the lonely roads on the moor that led from Postbridge to Two Bridges one evening when suddenly her car started to judder and came to a halt. She managed to pull over to the side of the road, and with concern, she pulled out the car handbook to try to determine what could be wrong with her car. What followed next would make her determined never to venture onto the moors at night again. "As I sat in the fading light, I suddenly felt very cold. It felt strangely like I was being watched. I looked up and suddenly saw these huge hairy hands outside the window of the car, pressing against it. I couldn't move. I couldn't scream. They were just there - so close to me. It was so horrible."

She watched in terror as the huge disembodied hairy hands crawled across the glass in front of her. "After what seemed like a lifetime, I heard myself scream and then the hands seemed to vanish."

She was so badly shaken that she hardly realised she had managed to start the car again, but as she drove away, she gradually started to think she must have imagined the whole thing. She had never heard of the ghostly giant hairy hands that have appeared to many others before her on the moor. She had not been the first to be become victim to such a frightening encounter. It seems the 'curse' of the road started back in 1921, when a soldier reported that a giant pair of hairy hands with long dark hair covering them, had literally taken over his steering wheel, the hands laying themselves on top of his own hands. Around the same time, a cyclist felt his handlebars ripped from his bicycle by huge hair-covered hands that appeared out of no-where. It caused him to smash straight into a wall alongside the road.

On another occasion, a doctor travelling by motorbike along the same road on the empty moors, had his engine detached from the motorbike, nearly killing him as he crashed. It was well-known along that barren countryside way, that horses would frequently bolt here, throwing their owners to the ground along this road.

In 1924, a young couple were visiting the moors on holiday in their camper van. As they reached this road, a heavy fog began to cover the ground and they decided to pull over and stop for the night rather than risk driving any further in the poor visibility.

They parked in a lay-by and made themselves some supper, and then settled down for the night in their sleeping bags. The female had only been asleep for a short while when she was woken by a strange scratching noise that seemed to be coming from outside the camper. Thinking it could be a lost dog out wandering in the cold on the moors, she climbed out of her sleeping bag and went toward the camper door to take a look. Suddenly a strange chill came over her, and she found herself instinctively turning to the nearest window. There, slowly crawling across the glass, was a giant pair of hands covered with long, thick shaggy dark hair. In absolute terror, frozen to the spot and unable to move, she made the sign of the cross and prayed aloud for help. To her tremendous relief, she watched as the hands slid off the windscreen and vanished. She spent the rest of the night unable to sleep and staring at the windscreen in case the hands re-appeared.

The local council, after a fair number of accidents, decided it was time to improve the road, believing quite naturally that if they improved the camber of the road, it would stop the accidents from occurring. However, after the road improvements had been carried out, strange things continued to occur. A few years later, a man was driving along the same road over the moors when something happened. He was found the next day, dead, lying underneath his car. His death was investigated, of course, but there seemed to be no cause for his death and when investigators examined his car, they could find nothing wrong with it. Locals of course whispered to each other about the probable cause of his unexplained demise....

## Chapter Nine:

## Folie a dieux

In 2008, an astonishing incident was captured live on CCTV, and also by a BBC film crew who just happened to be filming a documentary about the British motorway police. Two women are observed on the live screens at the M6 Motorway traffic control room in a rural part of Northern England near Stoke on Trent. They are walking along the central reservation of the motorway. The control room dispatches highway patrol officers to the scene, to stop the women; what they are doing is not only completely illegal, but it's also a highly dangerous and illogical place to be walking.

As the highway patrol car arrives at the scene and the officers get out of the car and begin to approach the women, back at the control room, the live screen shows both women climbing over the short barriers of the central reservation, then running straight into the path of the fast-flowing traffic on the motorway.

One of the women is hit by a car in the fast lane. However, despite having just been hit head-on by the car, inexplicably, she immediately gets straight back up and continues on running to the other side of the road. She seems to be completely oblivious to any pain.

Immediately, the control room call the motorway police to go to the scene. The BBC film crew from the control room also go in the car with the two police officers, filming their arrival as they go. They arrive within moments and are expecting to find the woman who was hit by the speeding car very seriously injured and needing urgent medical treatment.

As the police car and film crew pull up, the police officers get out of the car and approach the two women. The two women see the police and they suddenly become visibly agitated. As the police approach them and start to talk to them by the roadside, the BBC cameras capture the astonishing moment that one of the women side-steps the police and runs straight into the oncoming traffic, again, followed quickly after by her sister, who does exactly the same thing.

One of them is hit by a car and sent flying over its roof. The other is hit head-on by a lorry.

The police immediately call for an ambulance, stating to the emergency services over the walkie-talkie that it's probably going to be two fatalities; the women were both hit at full impact by the speeding vehicles.

The woman hit by the car, at a speed of at least 60 mph, is lying unconscious in the middle of the traffic lane. The woman hit by the lorry has broken bones visibly sticking out of her legs.

As the police go to her aid, she's heard saying, "I know you are not real." Then she starts becoming very aggressive, and even though her legs are busted, she becomes increasingly violent.

"I can't understand it," says the attending police officer Paul Finlayson. "For a person to survive being hit by a lorry is very, very rare. Seeing her thrown violently, seeing her run over by the wheels; no human was going to survive that." And yet she did. PC Cope, also at the scene said, "What I couldn't understand is that I've got a person who is smashed from the waist down but from the waist up is extremely aggressive, spitting, shouting, screaming. You start to wonder; what's going on here? It was very, very strange."

Then, still on camera, the woman who has been hit by the car, suddenly regains consciousness, seems to be in no pain at all, stands up, and punches a policewoman in the face, knocking her to the floor!

The policewoman is visibly incredulous afterward. As the BBC films it, she says, "I can't understand what's going on. I saw the car hit her; it threw her in the air like a doll."

The same woman then runs off and climbs over the central reservations barrier again and again runs into the oncoming traffic on the other side of the motorway. This time she's not run over, but she is trying to flee into the woods that run parallel to the road. She acts as if she has no injuries at all.

It takes six police, along with many concerned members of the public, who've got out of their cars to help, to restrain her, and she's threatening violence to them all!

"Her strength was phenomenal," says PC Cope. "She's got incredible strength. It's inexplicable. Both of them appeared to demonstrate such intense focus. They just wanted to fight us. Why were they on the motorway? Why did they want to fight us? Why were they trying to commit suicide?" The policeman is simply stunned by their behaviour. As well as having inexplicable strength, both of them also appeared to be absolutely terrified of the police, irrationally so it would seem as the police were simply trying to calm them down and protect them from harm and the police kept telling them they were there to help them.

The women's responses to this were bizarre to say the least. Their responses included screaming, "You are not the police," "What country do they come from?" "You are not real," "You cannot protect us", and one sister was screaming to the other one, "They want our body parts!"

Both women are eventually restrained and subdued and taken to hospital, but the woman hit by the car is released quickly and taken to the police station where she is charged with trespass and assaulting a police officer.

What no-one at the police station could understand however was why she seemed not to be physically injured in any way at all. She'd been thrown over the roof of a speeding car, and yet she was physically fine. The police also remarked how strange it was that she didn't once ask at all about the health of her sister, who'd been rushed to hospital. In fact, her entire demeanour had suddenly changed from one of extreme aggression and suspicion to one of friendliness and almost flirtatiousness.

It was suggested later by observers that she must have been given tranquilizers at the hospital; but she wasn't given any, and interestingly, the police found no evidence of any drugs in her system. They also found no record of any mental illnesses. Some observers of the film footage have since speculated, that they must have taken some kind of strong drug such as PCP or 'Bath Salts,' but again, no drugs were found in their systems. People suggested that the sisters must be on steroids then; but again, they had no traces of any mood or mind-altering drugs in their bodies.

The two women turned out to be identical twins of Swedish nationality, who allegedly between them had only one passport. It transpired that the women had been refused re-admittance to a public coach they had been travelling on after it had stopped for a refreshment break at the nearby service station. The coach driver believed he had seen them acting 'very suspiciously,' and as a result of his observations, he informed the manager of the service station.

The manager of the service station observed the sisters herself and believed they were carrying their bags very close to their chests and were conferring with each other, and in the manager's words, she thought it looked almost as though they were plotting something. The manager said she became concerned that there could be a bomb in their bags, so she called the police and the police arrived. However, the police could not find anything that concerned them and so they let the women go. The women were refused re-admittance to their coach however by the coach driver, and so it would seem that this was the most likely the reason why they were wandering along the motorway, albeit in a highly dangerous manner.

Fast forward past the scenes of them being hit by the vehicles on the motorway, and now the sister at the police station is being charged for assault. She's still being filmed. One of the policemen says to the camera, "She behaved as though nothing had ever happened, or as though she had no recollection of what had transpired. You can honestly say that person; that screaming banshee of a woman, is not the person that we picked up from the hospital. She's not exhibited any aggression. I was quite happy that she could be conveyed without being handcuffed." Which seems remarkable, but he continues, "It was the little things that bothered her, like what she looks like and what she's going to wear. She's not asked about her sister once, and that surprised me from start to finish dealing with her: It's as if her sister doesn't exist anymore. I don't think she knew anything that had gone on. She either didn't care, or she didn't remember."

"She was almost jolly, even flirtatious. With her it clearly worked to be pleasant with her, to flirt with her," the custody Sergeant noted, which is a bizarre thing for a policeman to say, but it seems she had somehow almost charmed him.

As she's being charged with the assault on camera, she's heard remarking that in her native country, "We say an accident rarely comes alone; usually at least one more follows."

Why would she make this statement? Well, in hindsight, it seems that she was perhaps sending a message about what her next intentions were, but no-one took any notice of the comment.

When the story hit all the National newspapers shortly after the next set of events transpired, no-one could understand how it was that she was not only physically unharmed and seemed impervious to pain, but that she was then released from police custody after only a few hours. She'd endangered her own life several times as well as the lives of others. Was she mentally fit to be out in general population?

What followed next was another highly mysterious chain of events. She was released the next day, and she found her way into the small rural town nearest to the police station. She is next seen by two men in the early summer evening, standing in the middle of the road as they walked along it. They'd just left the local Pub they frequently went to in the evenings for a beer and a chat. As the men left the Pub and entered the street, they couldn't fail to notice her standing in the middle of the road, and she called over to them, telling them how nice the dog was that they had with them. The two men strolled over to her so she could make a fuss of the dog and they got into a conversation. She explained that she was looking for her sister who was in hospital and also for a Bed and Breakfast hotel where she could stay the night.

One of the men, Glenn Hollinshead, pointed out to her that the small village she was in didn't really have any Bed and Breakfasts in it, but he suggested she go back with them to his house and he would make them all a bite to eat and then help her find her sister and a place to stay.

"We'd often sit in the pub and talk about his days in the Royal Air force and other chat," his friend Pete recalled. "As we started to walk home, you couldn't miss her, she stuck out with the big coat she was wearing and carrying all her possessions in a big transparent bag. She seemed a bit lost, unfocussed. Part of me was thinking: something's not right here. Why has she got all her possessions with her? Glenn was being a Good Samaritan, he was just trying to help her. Her personality opened up as we walked and she was really friendly. Back at the house, we were having beers and I asked her what happened to her sister and she went cold and changed. In the quiet moments between conversations she was getting paranoid and getting up and looking through the curtains out onto the street. She got her cigarettes out and offered them to us and we took one each, but just as we were about to light them she snatched them back and said we couldn't have them because they might be poisoned. I thought, is she hiding from someone? Glenn was more relaxed about the whole thing though." Glenn thought she was perhaps just a bit introverted, and he felt sorry for her and let her spend the night there at his house.

The following day, she stabbed him to death. He managed to make it out the front door and tell his neighbour she had stabbed him, but tragically he died shortly after. She fled the scene immediately.

British Army soldier Josh Grattage, driving in a street near-by, saw a woman walking along the pavement, smashing a hammer into her own head. "I was seeing lots of blood on her head. I felt a sickening feeling," he later told reporters. He slammed on his brakes and rushed to stop her hitting herself, only for her to pull part of a brick out of her pocket and hit him over the head with it, momentarily stunning him, and she ran away. It was of course the same woman who'd just killed Glenn.

She was finally spotted again and chased by the police on foot as she headed toward a bridge. Without hesitating, she jumped straight off the bridge and fractured her skull and her ankles. Later, she was jailed for the killing of Mr Hollinshead. It was 2010 and her name was Sabina Erikson. She was released on parole in 2011, just one year later. This would seem a remarkably short sentence. Additionally, due to the very evident display of her propensity to self-harm, it's absolutely astounding that she wasn't sentenced to a Mental Institution instead of Prison. Of her startling behaviour on the motorway, two psychiatrists deemed her to have experienced a sudden but brief and temporary outburst of madness.

"The mental illness resolved itself quickly," said one of the Judges in court, by way of explanation. "It had a sudden onset and resolved rapidly." If that was indeed the case, how did they know it would not resurface again in the future? And, how did her sister also happen to experience the exact same "sudden onset" of "temporary madness" at exactly the same time? It wasn't just this which was so strange. Why did they both have a seeming inability to feel any pain? The footage of their actions on the motorway that day has been available on the internet for years now, and many have speculated that if it wasn't drugs that caused their behavior, which it wasn't because none were found in their systems, and if neither of them had ever had a history of mental illness, then they must have become demon-possessed: that a demon must have taken control of their bodies and minds; driving them to commit these desperate acts of self-annihilation, with seemingly supernatural strength; urging them on to kill themselves, telling them to do it. Is this why they repeatedly threw themselves in front of speeding cars, and why Sabina was hitting her own head with a hammer? No matter our natural skepticism, accounts of demon possession go back to antiquity. And yet, both of them demon- possessed at the same time? So suddenly and explosively? Is that really in any way plausible?

Others suggested they act as though something else had taken control of their minds; that they have been 'mind-controlled' to kill themselves; to self-destruct on triggered command, and that to try to stop the voice in her head, Sabrina was hitting herself over the head with the hammer to drown out the voice issuing instructions. Mind control, as outlandish as it sounds, has been a favoured experiment for some governments in the past.

A U.S. Dr Ross Adey of 'Project Pandora,' allegedly conducted 'behaviour modification experiments,' using ELF frequency that 'caused frenzied emotional imbalance' in the people who were experimented on. Dr Michael Persinger, an expert in behavioural neuroscience, once boasted he could himself quite confidently control every brain on the planet. When MK Ultra was uncovered, 149 sub-projects were operating on College Campuses across the Unites States. Martin Cannon who wrote 'The Controllers', claimed to have read over 200,000 pages of documents from organizations including the CIA, and the Department of Defence, as well as witness testimonies, and from this, he believed he had found evidence that a person's mind could be controlled so that they believed they had gone through an encounter with alien entities. "Evidence exists linking members of the Intel community; CIA, Naval Intelligence, DARPA, with esoteric technology of mind control... For decades, 'spychiatrists' have been working behind the scenes - on college campuses. They have experimented with the erasing of memory, hypnotic resistance to torture, hypnotic suggestion, microwave induction of "voices," and a host of even more disturbing tech." Had these two women been subject to some kind of experimentation?

"Their behaviour was "Self-Terminate. Do not get captured," says conspiracy researcher Miles Johnston of the Bases Project. It is true the women were terrified of the police, and yet they had no known reason to be running from them, and they did say some very strange things to the police officers. They were scared, and running. But from what or whom?

"They have been underground," says Johnston, and points to their shouting, "You cannot protect us. They will take our Organs." He has spent over two decades interviewing witnesses of secret Military/Government Underground Bases, Johnston and his followers believe there is a lot more to this story than has been released. They believe the women were part of a growing number of 'MILAB's,' Military Abductees taken to underground bases and kept there for experimentation, and these two women, he suggests, could have been genetically experimented on; their DNA altered and their bodies 'modified and enhanced,' with the use of advanced alien technology, but done at the hands of human collaborators. The purpose? To create programmed assassins who feel no pain, are as such 'rechargeable,' and ultimately disposable after they have served their purpose. When in disposable phase, it is then that the thoughts of 'Self-Terminate' are sent into their heads.

Isn't this all just sci-fi fantasy though? And yet, it was almost as though Sabina had been programmed to go from suicidal self-destruct mode on the motorway, to flirtatious charmer in the police station where she seemingly captivated the policemen; to her sudden murderous outburst the following day, followed by further suicide attempts.

This sounds like mental illness, surely? And as some professionals in the psychiatric community said, it was simply an exceptionally rare 'folie a dieux,' a moment of shared madness, which came and went equally as fast.

Were these two sisters quite simply going into meltdown? Yet they seemed afraid of being captured, of going back to have their 'organs taken.'

Very strangely, a journalist called David McCann claimed to have looked into the case and he came up with the theory that the sister at Glenn's house did not carry out the murder at all: that other people did, who entered the house and took advantage of her mental illness and used it as a front to commit the murder and blame it on her. The problem with this is it lacks the evidence; however, the really odd thing is that he once used to post all over the internet, under various aliases, claiming that these genetically-enhanced mind-controlled 'super-soldiers' were real and did exist. Then, he investigates this case of these two Swedish women and openly states these hybrid tortured genetically MILAB abducted super-soldiers don't exist; he was wrong. How strange that he now has changed his mind completely! Why would he do that? Should we read more into this? Or simply pass it all off as not just a folie a dieux, but the madness of many ....?

# Chapter Ten:

# Hecate in the ancient Woods

The 'Clapham Woods Mystery' refers to an ancient woodland area in West Sussex, England, where many believe satanic and other-worldly activity has been occurring for a very long time, and that within this wood lies the answers to the strange phenomenon of disappearing dogs and people too.

For many who have gone to the ancient woodland, they say it is imbued with an eerie atmosphere, and a nauseating sensation often comes over those who wander in the woods there. The creeping sensation of someone or something following them is an oft-reported phenomenon. Even the sensations of being pushed by something unseen, while dogs have a habit of disappearing in the woods, never to be seen again. Policeman Peter Goldsmith's body was found hidden amongst the trees in 1972. A Vicar was found dead after disappearing in the woods there.

Occult investigators Charles Walker and Toyne Newton detailed their own investigation of the woods in 1987, after they had carried out a comprehensive on-site stake-out investigation over several months.

Walker said that during this period, he put notices in the local newspapers, appealing for information from the general public about any strange goings-on in the woods. Among the replies he received was a very intriguing one. A person wrote to him saying that he had something of interest to tell him but he must meet him in the woods. On the alloted evening, Walker set off for the woods with slight trepidation and as he waited alone in the dark woods, he began to wonder why he had so readily agreed to this arrangement. The person duly arrived; but they would not show their face. It was a man and he warned Walker; do not turn around to look at me. The man was masked behind a tree. The man said he belonged to a group who had 'friends in high places,' and that Walker must cease all further investigation into the woods, or there would be serious repercussions. This group, the man said, worshipped the diety Hecate, Queen of the dark moon, and his friends, he warned Walker, "would tolerate no interference" in their ritualistic killings. Says Walker, cryptically, "The human disappearances, of which there were several, ended up as 'open verdicts.' Searches were made of the likely routes, paths these people were thought to have taken, and nothing was found. Then sometime later, bodies were found in areas known to have been extensively searched by the Police."

In other words, it would seem that the bodies were kept, either alive or dead, for some time, prior to being placed back at a spot where they were most likely to be discovered laying there blatantly out on display on an open path....

# Chapter Eleven:

# The Island Mystery

It's a mystery that has puzzled, perplexed and baffled both experts and amateur sleuths combined, ever since it happened.

A man's body is found up on a hill, four months after he disappeared on the Isle of Mull. He was last seen getting into his private plane. His body was found with only a tiny scratch, but his body hadn't been where it was found when all the search parties had looked for him, multiple times. Then his body was found, where searchers had looked. What happened to Peter Gibbs? And how did his body get to where it was found?

The man in question was Norman Peter Gibbs, known as Peter. He was a talented violinist and from the 1950's to the 1970's he'd been Head of BBC Northern Ireland Symphony Orchestra as well as leader of BBC Scotland's Orchestra. He'd been a fighter pilot in World War II with RAF 41 Squadron. After the War, he had his private Tiger Moth plane modified so that he could fit his violin into the baggage compartment.

His comrades in the RAF called him 'a daredevil' and a plain talking man, while those who knew him from the orchestra described him as a practical joker, such as the time he flew over a live Orchestra performance and 'bombed' them all with bags of flour.

While playing for the Philharmonic orchestra in Washington D.C., he stood up to chastise the German conductor, who it was believed had joined the Nazi party during the War, although no doubt he had no choice in this matter. Gibbs addressed the conductor in front of the rest of the orchestra for his arrogance and rudeness, which Gibbs had not been alone in noticing.

The conductor in response demanded an apology and refused to perform again until Gibbs was sacked. The orchestra refused to back the German conductor however, and Gibbs played on for the rest of the tour, while the

German and his lawyers left to take up a new position at the Berlin and Vienna Philharmonics orchestra.

Gibbs, whose body was later to be inexplicably found up a hill on the Isle of Mull, went on to form the 'Peter Gibbs quartet,' which according to musician David Myers was a rather Avant guarde affair. One of the violinists in his Quartet was a man called Carter, who remarked, "Being made up of very talented young musicians it was immediately successful, but Gibbs being Gibbs, he demanded such high standards of them that it inevitably disbanded." Perhaps the reason for this was that Gibbs had insisted each member should sit in different corners of the room with their backs to each other and start playing by some sort of intuition! "This and many other crazy ideas proved too much for the others, who all left."

According to Peter Mountain, who played in the London Symphony Orchestra with Gibbs, on one occasion Gibbs was getting a lift to the orchestra performance with another member, Rodney Friend, when they got caught up in traffic that had ground to a halt at Hyde Park Corner in the centre of London, in the middle of rush hour. They would be late to their performance at the Royal Albert Hall if the traffic did not shift. Rather than resigning themselves to this fate, Gibbs asked to sit in the driver's seat whereupon he drove into the oncoming traffic lane, shot into the Park where cars were not allowed, came out the other end, shot through red traffic lights, and "nonchalantly parked outside the Artists entrance!" It would seem then, that Gibbs was a man full of zest, a spirit of adventure and much daring.

During his time in the Orchestras, he had also been flying privately. In 1957, he joined the Surrey Flying Club, and had been flying private airplanes ever since. He owned a De Havilland Tiger Moth.

Not only was Gibbs a fearless daredevil, but he was ambitious too. While still head of BBC Scotland's Orchestra, he began to make money as a property developer, and in 1975 he finally left his professional musician's career and began to expand his property development business. He was doing very well and making good money, and he had great plans. One of these plans was a little unusual, although not completely unique. He wanted to buy a hotel and build a private landing strip beside it so that wealthy guests could arrive directly by private jet.

On Christmas Eve 1975, he travelled to Scotland. He was accompanied by his girlfriend Felicity Grainger. It would be his birthday the following day, Christmas Day. He planned to stay on the Isle of Mull to celebrate. The Isle of Mull is a small island of the Inner Hebrides and lies off the west coast of Scotland. It is comprised of just 338 square miles, with a population of under 3,000.

Gibbs flew himself and Felicity to the Island in his private plane, landing on the small airstrip not far from the hotel, The Glenforsa, where they had booked to stay. A small number of hotels in the US and the Bahamas had a private landing strip, as Gibbs envisaged building, but so too did this hotel, The Glenforsa, although the private landing strip was only allowed to be used in daylight hours, as it had no lights. It also did not have all the usual accompaniments such as traffic control, and radar. For this reason, the hotel only gave permission for planes to land during fair weather and daylight, and only in the spring and summer months.

The landing strip known as Glenforsa Airfield is located on the north coast of the Island, beside the hotel. The runway is a grass strip 780 metres by 28 metres. The length is level, but the width has a slight slope down to the sea. Pilots are warned; Livestock may be on the airstrip from October to April, and Geese may present a hazard throughout the year. Turbulence can be expected on approaches with strong southerly winds. A curved approach should be made, due to the high terrain. The Glenforsa itself is a Norwegian wooden log hotel, from which outdoor pursuits include bird watching and hill walking. It is set amid an ancient landscape with many Standing Stones and Cairns.

On Christmas Eve, Gibbs and his girlfriend flew from North Connel airfield, near Oban in Western Scotland, where Gibbs had hired a two-seater Cessna 150H light aircraft, registration G-AVTN, equipped with navigation and communication equipment, but not equipped with parachutes. This was normal. It would have been very unusual for parachutes to be carried in any model of the modern light aircrafts, experts would later say.

Later that morning, Gibbs flew Felicity to the Isle of Skye with him, where they checked out a few of the hotels, in view of his property development plans. On the afternoon of the 24th, Gibbs flew them back to the Isle of Mull, landing just before 4 pm, just as it was beginning to get dark. So far, all was well.

They ate in the hotel restaurant that evening, during which they shared a bottle of red wine, and some reports say whiskey too. By all accounts from the hotel staff, Gibbs was in a great mood that evening, although he did express disappointment that it seemed he would not be able to fly on his birthday, Christmas Day, as a storm was due to come in.

At around 9 pm, when they were still seated in the hotel restaurant, Gibbs apparently suddenly decided he would fly tonight instead. He had a plan – he wanted to see if it was possible to land on the hotel airstrip in the dark.

He quickly left his chair and returned to his room, where he changed into his flying gear, then returned to the dining room and requested that his girlfriend come outside with him, armed with two torches to use as make-shift landing lights to guide him home. He asked her to follow him outside and wait on the landing strip for him, with the two torches placed on either side of the landing strip to show him where it was in the dark.

As hotel staff overheard his plans, they offered their opinion on this folly and strongly tried to persuade him against this rash idea. It was not allowed, they said, and of course, they could immediately see the danger in this experiment. Gibbs responded by informing them that he was not asking for their permission – merely telling them of his decision. He explained to them briefly that he was a highly competent and experienced pilot, and there was no risk because his girlfriend Miss Grainger would be guiding him back inland with the torch lights. This would then prove to him whether he would be able to go ahead with the plan for buying a hotel himself, and having a landing strip put in, that could be used day or night.

He'd been a fighter pilot in the Royal Air Force in World War II, so this quick night-time flight was hardly going to faze him, presumably. Besides which, the flight would be over and done with in the space of a few minutes.

So, he went ahead, going out to his small plane and starting it up. Felicity sat in the plane with him as it taxied along the landing strip, and then he stopped to let her out.

As he took to the sky in his plane, his girlfriend/assistant duly placed the two lit torches at the end of the grass landing strip, pointing out toward the sea. Then, there she stood, in the cold and the wind, awaiting his return.

She waited for an hour. He should have returned within five minutes or so. He never returned.

Despite an ensuing huge air, sea and land search, no trace of him nor his plane were found. Of course, the most logical explanation was that he tragically, for some reason, crashed his plane into the sea. Perhaps it had been engine failure, or it was pilot error of some kind, and terribly sadly, the pilot and his plane had sunk into the depths of the ocean. This would completely explain why he was not found: he was now lying dead at the bottom of the sea.

The Island itself was searched, in case they were wrong, but no sign of him or his plane were found, despite the police and hundreds of volunteers searching the remote barren and isolated land below his flight path, many times and most thoroughly, and the RAF and Navy Air Service helicopters scoured the island for any sign of the plane wreck and Gibbs.

However, this is not the end to the story – it really is just the beginning, and yet the end is also cryptically unfinished. You see, four months after that fateful night on Christmas eve, in April 1975 a shepherd called Donald MacKinnon stumbled across Gibbs' dead body. It was lying on a hillside overlooking the sound of Mull and Pennygown Cemetery, less than a mile from the grass airstrip from which Gibbs had taken off.

He was lying on his back across a log. The owner of the hotel, David Howitt saw the body in-situ and he immediately confirmed that the body was wearing the clothes and flying boots that Peter Gibbs had been wearing on the evening he disappeared. It looked as though he had simply lain down there and died, he said.

Gibbs was entirely alone. There was no plane wreckage around him. His body was pristine save for a tiny cut on his leg. He did not look at all like a victim of a catastrophic plane crash. He did not look like someone who had plummeted to the ground from a plane, nor crashed into the sea, escaped from his plane in the icy winter waters, swum inland, and climbed his way onto land, then succumbed to his injuries and died.

His body was taken away for medical examination by Dr W.D.S. McLay, chief medical Officer of Strathclyde Police, and Gibbs' death was ruled by the coroner as having been caused by "Exposure." After his body was discovered, search parties went out again across the Island, dragging the inland lochs and searching through woods for the plane wreckage again, but no wreckage could be found.

Was it at all possible he had swum ashore, in temperatures as low as 6 degrees centigrade, where the life-expectancy for survival in the water was under an hour? It would seem, even for a former World War II fighter pilot, to have been a feat of superhuman endeavour; although his son says he was shot down four times by the Germans during World War II and survived.

His son said that what his father did that night, attempting to fly inland with no navigation and no landing strip lights, was quite in keeping with his father's personality. What's perhaps most pertinent here though, is that in order for

Gibbs to have got to the hill where he was found, he would have had to cross over the road which led directly to the hotel. Why wouldn't he have seen the hotel lights and headed for the shelter of the hotel? Why wouldn't he have headed along the road with the intention of reaching warmth and safety inside the hotel, rather than climb a hill? If Gibbs had the astonishing ability to climb free of his watery grave and make it back to shore intact, why would he then cross the road and climb 400ft up a hill to die of exposure, when all he had to do was follow that road and the lights back to the Hotel?

Gibbs' son Alan is not convinced his father swam to shore and climbed up to his death. When speaking to the BBC he said that he recreated the route his father took that night. "There's almost a continuous vertical wall of rock; some of it is two metres high, some of it's three metres high, and there are relatively few gaps. Now this is the climb that I attempted in the company of my husky, who's pretty eager and pulls pretty hard. In about 40 minutes, I got half-way to where the body was found. There were points where I had to turn around and go back. It was boggy. I could not make it myself, in daylight. I would stake every bit of my reputation that nobody swam directly to shore and climbed up that hill in the dark."

If Gibbs had been climbing vertically on rocks, in the dark, with water-filled boots and heavy wet jacket, how could he have made it? And how did he have no scratches or bumps or marks on his body?

The coroner said that his body was, "Entirely consistent with lying there for a period of four months," which was the amount of time between him disappearing and being found, and yet what is very odd is that he had no sea salt on his body. Surely that would be completely impossible, given that he had supposedly swum back to shore?

The explanation given was that he had lain there so long, the elements had removed all traces; but wouldn't the winds on the exposed island, surrounded by the sea, be full of sea salt? Forensic tests on Gibbs body detected no marine organisms at all, neither on his body nor his clothes or the boots he still wore. No matter how heavy the rain might have been in the four months he was said to have been lying there, how could there be no traces of sea water in his boots, which would have been saturated, had he swum ashore?

Then there is the inexplicable condition of his body. It was entirely intact, with no injuries whatsoever apart from a tiny scratch on his leg. His plane was still missing, and so no other conclusion could be given other than that it had crashed, and as the entire island had been searched for the wreckage, it must be in the sea; but a crash surely would have caused him injuries? Wouldn't he have been in a

frantic, desperate struggle to eject himself from the plane while underwater, and wouldn't that seem impossible to do without causing more than a tiny scratch to himself? Wouldn't he have fought with all his might to free himself from the plane wreck as it sunk to the depths? He couldn't have jumped from the plane mid-air; for he had no parachute.

Then, in September 1986, almost a decade after Gibbs' body had been found, two brothers, Richard and John Grieve were clam diving in the Sound of Mull, when they discovered a wreckage at a depth of 100 feet. This was about a mile to the east of the direct approach to the grass landing strip. It was Gibbs' plane. When the wreckage was inspected underwater, it appeared the plane had crashed with some impact. The engine was detached from the airframe and lying some distance from it. One of the aircraft's wheels was missing. The wings were also detached. The front perspex screen was shattered. Both doors of the plane were still locked. Escape could only have been achieved through the shattered perspex screen, by climbing through sharp jagged edges. Wouldn't this have been very difficult to do, in a rush to get to the surface, without some injury at least to the body? The islanders were baffled.

For some reason, the plane was not recovered, and the photos the clam brothers had taken of the wreckage were not good enough to allow expert air-accident inspectors to assess whether the crash had been survivable. Local man Richard Grieve, when talking to Ian Punnit of the BBC said he found it implausible to believe that Gibbs swam back to shore. He said he himself uses an 8mm thick dry suit whenever he enters the icy waters that surround the water. "I wouldn't like to swim in that even in my dry-suit. When he got ashore, why would he cross a road and walk up a steep hill; it just doesn't make sense. I just don't see that what came up in the official reports could be true. I was talking to some farmers and on the night of the crash they said they heard a plane go up over their farm. There was some talk about him going to Northern Ireland, something to do with the IRA. That would have taken about an hour, hour and a half. You'd have thought the authorities would lift the plane, for all it would have taken; all you would need is a couple of airbags. I doubt the official story – there's too many things that don't ring true. The more I think of it, the more I doubt it."

Retired engineering academic Alan Organ, who has dedicated many years to looking into this mystery, said it was simply impossible to jump from anything higher than 10 feet without very serious injury or death.

After Gibbs' body had been found lain on the log, a fatal accident enquiry had been held on the mainland in Oban on June the 24th 1976, minus the plane. The enquiry, and the following media coverage seemed only to raise even more anomalies. The local shepherd who had stumbled across Gibbs' body was very forthright in stating that he and his sheepdog had walked past the spot where the body was discovered on multiple occasions after Gibbs had disappeared, and he had never seen the body there in all that time.

He insisted: the man's body was not there, and this was backed-up by Mountain Rescue teams who had also searched the exact area several times and seen no body there, as had all the volunteers. The Islanders were shocked and confused by this. They also expressed surprise that his body was completely intact. They knew from past experience and from being very familiar with the environment that bodies left out in the wild Scottish Highlands and Islands, whether human or animal, stood a very slim chance of not being picked at by natural predators. Very strangely, this was not the case for Gibbs' body. It had suffered no predation, and this they felt was extremely odd, given that it was supposed to have been lying there for four months.

David Howitt, for Mull historical and archaeological society said, "In my experience as a farmer, any corpses lying around, whether cattle, sheep, or deer, are soon attacked by scavengers and reduced to piles of bones," and he adds, "Robert Duncan told me that he had been past that place several times with his dogs in the intervening period and found nothing. The huge land and air search in the days following the disappearance also drew a blank."

Cryptically he says, "One wonders how much experience the pathologists had of bodies exposed for such periods. Supposing they had reported that its condition was not consistent with this period of exposure, what would the repercussions have been? Best to give the expected answer and allow the whole tragic affair to be quietly forgotten..."

Speculation and rumour was that Gibbs' body could have been dumped there at some time after his death, despite the medical examiner's ruling that he had been there for four months. Some suggested he must have been on a clandestine mission for MI6 in Northern Ireland. He had worked and lived in Ireland while playing violin for BBC Ireland Orchestra. 'The troubles' in Northern Ireland were ongoing, and so this speculative theory grew wings with the suggestion that the IRA had captured him then returned him to the Island after killing him, to leave a calling card, to taunt the powers-that-be that the IRA would not be messed with. Wouldn't this seem quite an exotic theory though? There was also nothing about Gibbs that would have suggested he could have been involved in terrorists and spy activities.

Perhaps he was smuggling something precious and illicit? And yet again, there was never any suggestion that Gibbs was anything more than a Patriot who had fought for his country's freedom, and an honest man, so it would seem improbable that he was up to no good, and how would that explain his death anyway? Had he been trying to fake his own death and it had gone horribly wrong? Had it been some kind of insurance scam gone wrong? And yet, if so, why would he end up on a log on a hill with four months of time missing between his disappearance and his subsequent discovery? There was also nothing in his commercial life that suggested anything other than an honest and successful businessman. Did he have another, secret yet unfathomable reason to attempt what most pilots would say was a lunatic plan to land in the dark, other than to see if it could be done? After all, if it could be done, surely he would still have been hard pressed to find other private charter pilots willing to gamble their lives on seeing if they too could land in the dark on a tiny airstrip with no lights or navigational aids, all for the purpose of staying at a hotel? Why would any other pilots be willing to possibly and quite probably crash and die by flying to a hotel that required blind night-time landing on a grass strip without lights?

The purpose of Gibbs' planned idea was for luxury guests to come to a hotel he would purchase, not suicidal private charter pilots or passengers. It was later discovered that when Gibbs hired the private plane to fly to Mull, his pilot's license had actually expired, although he did have over 2,000 hours of flying experience. To Gibbs though, this was not such a reckless or suicidally risky plan. According to the research of David Byers, former Chief Producer of Music & Arts for the BBC, on one occasion, and it was to be only once for good reason, businessman and Stradivarius violin owner Morrison Dunbar was invited by Gibbs to fly from Glasgow airport over Loch Lomond and the Trossachs National Park in the Highlands of Scotland.

Said Dunbar afterwards; "It immediately became clear that Peter was navigating solely by means of a small AA Handbook." In other words, he was navigating his plane using an Automobile Association road map! "When he got lost, he would fly down and take a quick look at the road signs!" Gibbs was no doubt a true daredevil, but what has never been solved is the mystery of how his body ended up where it did.

Curiously, it was alleged that while his girlfriend Felicity was awaiting the arrival of the police after Gibbs failed to return, she mentioned that he had told her; "If everything went wrong, he would throttle back and jump to safety."

Well again, jumping on land, no matter how low, would have resulted in some form of injury to his body, and the plane did not land on the island; it landed in the sea, and the belief that he somehow managed to swim in the freezing water with both his water-logged boots and heavy flying jacket, would surely seem an impossible feat?

Why would an experienced albeit dare-devil pilot even want to have to jump out of a plane in the pitch black on a winter's night, not even knowing if he were jumping into the sea or jumping onto land; either of which could have only spelt certain disaster and most probable death? He certainly did not come across as a man who had an overriding death-wish. None of his friends said he was in any way depressed. They could never imagine him wanting to commit suicide, they all said. No matter the practical joker that he was, he had great future plans in business, was a man of ambition and had made a great success of his life. He certainly never indicated to anyone who knew him that he wouldn't mind killing himself. Yet he must have known how dangerous it was to do what he was planning; so was there some other reason for it? What could that reason have possibly been? He knew he had no parachute in the aircraft.

Interestingly, the owners of the hotel, David and Pauline Howitt later claimed that while watching Gibbs manoeuver his plane before take-off, they had both seen two torches being moved separately at the end of the runway. This seemed to imply the presence of a third person on the runway, although Gibb's girlfriend Felicity maintained that only she handled both torches. Had it really been Gibbs at the controls that night some people wondered? Or had he planned his disappearance to escape a personal problem or business debts? And yet if he had planned to run-away from it all and start a new life, how did he end up dead up a steep hill four months after his plane vanished?

The locks were still in place when the aircraft was found. Does this mean sabotage and subterfusion of some kind had taken place?

The medical examiner did not see Gibbs' body in situ. He received the body for post-mortem on the mainland. He found the whole thing rather curious. "He was clothed, and I just found this a very odd problem to be faced with. It's weird that the body didn't turn up fairly quickly after the crash; that's very unusual and one would expect fairly major injuries coming out of a plane like that. There was nothing to suggest he had come out of a plane flying at any speed at all. There was nothing to suggest he had died in one place and been taken and put in another place. There was a toxicology search for any poisons or medicines or alcohol and to the best of my recollection nothing was found by forensic scientists."

Had someone got in the plane, hijacked it, held him hostage, and somehow, he ends up dead on a hill having been kept somewhere else for four months? And yet, his girlfriend had taxied with him in the plane before he took off, and the medical examiner said he died on the hill.

A mystery passenger would have to have got in after she got out, and yet the owners of the hotel, other staff and several guests told reporters that they had watched him that night through the windows of the hotel, and no-one else could have been in the plane if his girlfriend had got in to taxi to the end of the grass landing strip, as the plane was just a two-seater. And, if he had been killed by a captor or captors, why not dispose of his body somewhere secret, where it would never be found, rather than put it somewhere in plain sight?

"In the absence of anything else," said the medical examiner, "We were reduced to saying he had died simply of exposure."

What happened that Christmas eve night when Gibbs took off on his daredevil mission? What happened to his body in the four months between when he disappeared and when he was found? Exactly how did he end up on that steep hill, dead?

## Chapter Twelve:

## American Dyatlov

I first wrote about this case back in 2017, because when I first came across it, I found it absolutely intriguing, and completely baffling.

"There was some force that made 'em go up there," Jack Madruga's mother Mabel says firmly. She is talking about the tragic and very strange death of her son and his friends in the middle of the wilderness.

Described by the Washington Post in 1978, as "The American Dyatlov Pass," it's a curious, bizarre, and ultimately tragic case of the mysterious unsolved death of five young men in the woods in the mountains of the Plumas National Forest. Their names were Bill Sterling, Jack Madruga, Gary Mathias, Ted Weiher, Jack Huett.

It had started out with five men – one was now missing and the other four were dead. One of the deceased men was found in a cabin. The cabin had enough food and fuel to heat it for several months - but this fuel was never used, and most of the food was uneaten, and the man found dead inside had lost 100 lbs. He had slowly starved to death. Strangely, he was also found wrapped in a shroud. Three of the other men were found at varying distances from the cabin, and in various conditions of death. For the Washington Post in 1978, Professor of Journalism Cynthia Gorney writes, 'There was a half-moon that night, a winter moon in a cloudless sky. Up in the mountains above Feather River, the snow-drifts sometimes rose to 15 feet.' It was February 24th, 1978. The five young men had left a basketball game at the California State University in Chico at 10 p.m., got into their Mercury Montego car and driven off. It was assumed that they were heading home. Three blocks away, they pulled over at a late-night store and bought 2 fruit pies, a Snickers, a Marathon, some milk and two Pepsi's.

They all lived at home, and although their families referred to them as "boys" they were grown men. Jackie Huett was the youngest at 24 and Ted Weiher the oldest, at 32. Three of the 'boys' had been diagnosed as being 'mentally retarded.' Jack Madruga had not been diagnosed but was 'slow' according to his mother. Gary Mathias had been taking medication for schizophrenia, which had been diagnosed 5 years ago, but his Doctor and family said this condition had not re-surfaced in the past 2 years as it was being successfully managed by his medication.

The boys had all been due to play in a basketball tournament the next day for the "Gateway Gators" as part of the Yuba city vocational rehabilitation centre for the handicapped. Yuba city lay between Plumas National Forest and Mendocino National Forest. That night however, none of them came home, and despite the families calling each other, no-one had any clue where the boys might be. They had never stayed out for the night.

"Ted wouldn't have missed that game for anything," his mother Mrs. Weiher said. "He'd gone to the Special Olympic play-off's in L.A. last year and had gotten autographs. He even had his basketball clothes all laid out in his room."

A subsequent intense and prolonged search for the five missing friends, by Sheriffs and relatives, proved fruitless.

A woman who wished to remain anonymous contacted the police to say that she had seen the five men outside Mary's Country Store in Brownsville; a small town more than an hour's drive over back country roads from Rogers Cow Camp where their vehicle would later be found abandoned. The woman did not report her information to Sheriffs until March the 3rd however, after missing persons posters had been circulated with pictures of the missing boys.

Lt. Dennis Moore of the County Sheriff's office said at the time that he believed she was "A credible witness and we take her information seriously." A search of the small town then followed. According to this witness, two of the men were in a pickup truck, another two of them were at the outside telephone booth, and the fifth man was inside the store. "I noticed them because they didn't look from this area and you notice strangers round here, especially with their big eyes and facial expressions," she said. But why would they be in a small town store miles from home?

A second person said she saw the five boys in a red 1950's pick-up truck at about 2 p.m. on Saturday February 25th, the day after they disappeared. But if they were in another vehicle, who owned this vehicle? And why did they get into it? Where was their car?

Then, four days after they went missing, more than an hour's drive away North West of the Oro-Quincy Highway by back country roads, and close to Rogers Cow Camp, Jack Madruga's '69 turquoise and white Mercury Montego was found abandoned. On the night they had gone missing, the snow in this location was waist-deep. As reporter Gorney wrote; 'From that day on, nothing they found, nothing anybody told them, seemed to make any sense.'

The car was 70 miles from the town of Chico, on 'a deserted and rut-ravaged mountain road.' Later, investigators would express their disbelief that the car could have even got to the location it was found in, without sustaining serious and irreparable damage. The car had stopped at the snow line, and although investigators could see that the car's tires had spun a little, the vehicle was not actually stuck in the snow; five strapping young men could very easily have dislodged it and driven on. The undercarriage of the car was undamaged, despite it having a low-hanging muffler, and despite it ending up on a stretch of extremely bumpy mountain road that they had driven on in complete darkness. For the life of them, the investigators could not understand how there were no dents no scratches no gouges or even layers of mud to show for it.

Just as curious, was why they would have driven there in the first place. The investigators' conclusion was that the car's driver had used the most astonishing precision, accuracy, and care, to drive the car there unscathed; or, the driver knew the road so well that they could navigate every single rut and hole and bump with laser-like accuracy; which seemed impossible, for the boys' parents said the boys had never gone to that area before, and they were not the outdoors adventurous type. It was not an expedition their parents would ever have dreamed them setting out on, particularly given their mild disabilities.

The families also said that only Jack Madruga ever drove his car. He would never let any of his friends drive it, ever, and his parents were adamant that he did not know that road, at all. And they added that he absolutely hated the cold. Bill Sterling's father said that he had taken his son fishing once at a cabin but his son had not enjoyed it at all, and from then on, over eight years earlier, Bill had never gone on any other outdoors trips. His parents still went –

but he would always stay home.

Another of the boys, Ted Weiher, had once gone deer hunting, but he too had not enjoyed it and had not wanted to go to the forest ever again according to his parents. Only Gary Mathias had ever stayed out all night a couple of times, with friends, but the others were really stay-at-home types who preferred stability and predictability and order in their daily lives. There wasn't anyone in their families who could fathom what would have taken them to that destination, all the way along that precarious road into the forest.

Said the LA Times, 'Families and friends of the men and Sheriffs' investigators find themselves grasping at the few hard facts in the case, constructing theories that sometimes collapsed with the surfacing of new clues. And what gnaws most desperately, they say, is that virtually none of the theories makes sense.'

As for the two witness sightings, it would have to have meant that the boys had left the car there on the snow line and somehow acquired a truck and driven to a small town an hour away that they did not know. And if they were calling anyone from that phone booth, why didn't they call their parents? Were the witnesses mistaken?

The boys' predicament was not a question of them running out of gas in Madruga's car. The gas tank was found to be still quarter full. The keys to the vehicle were gone, but when police attempted to hot-wire the car, the engine started on first try. There was nothing faulty with the car engine.

Inside the car glove compartment there were four maps, although they were neatly folded up and did not appear to have been opened. On the car seats were scattered wrappers of candy – from their purchases at the late-night store after leaving the basketball game.

Where their car was driven there, the snow had been six to eight feet deep. The terrain surrounding the car was rocky and mountainous and thick forest. It would have been pitch dark when they got there. They were not suitably dressed for walking anywhere in the snow; they were all wearing casual street clothes and low-cut shoes. No hats, no scarves, no boots. They all hated the cold and the wilderness, yet they had left their car. Why? And where were they now?

John Thompson, Special Agent from the California Department of Justice called the case simply, "Bizarre. There are no explanations." According to Deputy Sheriff Richard Stenberg, there was no evidence of foul play at the car's location, "The car was littered with candy wrappers, basketball programs, milk cartons, and other material indicating a good time. We found no trace of the men during a 5-day search of the surrounding area."

A snow storm laid almost ten inches of snow on the ground and searching was extremely difficult. Despite using snow-cats, it was hard to make progress, but the search team did their best; yet they found no signs of the five men who had been in the car.

Their abandoned car sat on a gravel recreational road northeast of Oroville in Butte County's rugged Rogers Cow Camp area. The site was at an elevation of 4,500 feet, and more than 2 hours from Chico by car, and far off the direct auto route between Chico and Marysville. The police discovered that Mathias knew people in Forbestown - about halfway between Chico and Yuba cities, and local people say that route is on a road with a turnoff that is so easy to miss, anybody driving it late at night, without good knowledge of the route might have ended up heading north, toward the mountains, and got lost. The thing was – these friends hadn't heard from Mathias in two years and he'd never gone up there by car to see them. He didn't even know the way.

It was not until June, four months after the Spring thaw, that a group of motorcyclists wandered across a deserted forestry service camper at the end of a service road, twenty miles from where the boys' car had been found. It was the smell that hit them first. On entering the trailer, the stench was overpowering, and they saw a body on a bed stretched out and covered up by sheets as though he had been wrapped up like a shroud. The body was later identified as one of the five missing men – it was Ted Weiher, and he had frozen to death.

Eight sheets had been pulled over his body and tucked around his head. He wore no shoes and his shoes appeared to be missing from the trailer. One of the other boys' sneakers, belonging to Mathias's, were there, and the investigators hypothesised that he may have swapped them for Weiher's leather shoes, possibly after he developing frostbite.

On a small table beside the bed lay the ring Weiher used to wear, along with a gold chain that was also his, and his wallet with cash still inside it. There was also a gold watch, but its crystal face was missing. The families of the five boys said that they did not recognise the watch and it was not believed to belong to any of them. Had a stranger been there with them? Or had it belonged to a forest ranger, months or years earlier, who had discarded it because it was broken?

"The sparse evidence so far uncovered indicates that at least one other of the missing men had also sought safety in the shelter then left it," reports said.

As for Ted Weiher underneath the shroud, his body was emaciated. He had lost approximately 100 pounds. He had also developed frostbite on his feet at some point. According to the coroner, the growth of his beard showed that he had lived inside this abandoned trailer, though slowly starving to death, for anywhere between 8 – 13 weeks.

Somehow, for some reason, he had managed to make it 20 miles from their abandoned car, in waist-deep snow, wearing just a thin shirt and lightweight pants. For some reason, he had left the safety and relative shelter of the car on that snowy ice-cold night and ended up at the trailer. How had he travelled on foot through snow that was up to six feet deep, for 20 miles in the pitch dark until he came to the abandoned trailer? He, or one of his friends, had broken into the trailer through a window.

Matches were found inside the trailer, but they had not been used to make a fire. There was also a pile of paperback novels and wood furniture – plenty to start a fire with. Yet no fire had been lit. A storage shed which sat next to the trailer had been opened and from this, at least 12 food ration cans had been opened and emptied. One was determined to have been opened using an army-issue can opener. Both Mathias and Madruga had served in the Army, so it was assumed by investigators that only they would have known how to use the army-standard can opener.

What hadn't been used was all the dehydrated food in a locker in that storage shed. Investigators found enough dehydrated dinners inside the locker to feed all five of the missing men for at least 1 year, yet they had not touched it. There was also another storage shed beside the trailer and this held a propane tank that could have been used to provide heating inside the trailer. Why had they not used any of this equipment or food?

"They could have had gas in the trailer," said lead investigator Lieutenant Lance Ayers. "All they had to do was turn that gas on, and they'd have had heat."

For Lieutenant Ayers, the search for the missing boys was more personal than most cases he dealt with. He had gone to school with one of them. According to reports, after finding no trace of the missing men in the forest, he had even chased up on leads given to him by psychics. He had driven around for days on one occasion, looking for a house described by a psychic, which she said the boys had been taken to and killed in – but he could find no such house.

Professor Emeritus at UC Berkley School of Journalism, Cynthia Gorney got a good sense of the missing boys back then during her in-depth research of the strange case. Ted Weiher had been friendly and was as trusting as a boy, she said. 'He waved at strangers and brooded for hours if they did not wave back.' He 'got a chuckle out of phoning Bill and reading oddball names from the phone book.' He'd had a couple of jobs, including janitor and snack bar server.

Jackie Huett 'looked after him in a protective way and would dial the phone for him when he had to make a call.' Jack Madruga, a school graduate and Army Veteran, had recently been laid off from his busboy job. William Sterling was Madruga's special friend. He was deeply religious and would spend hours reading literature aloud 'to bring Jesus to patients in mental hospitals.'

Gary Mathias, also an Army Vet, helped in his stepfather's gardening business. He'd received a medical discharge after drug and mental health problems emerged while he was serving overseas. On a couple of occasions it was said that he'd become aggressive and a little violent. Where was Mathias now? His father reported that his son had been taking his medicine weekly, as prescribed, and he had taken them now for 3 years for the treatment of schizophrenia, without any problems. His family said that while he had been in trouble overseas for fighting before he was diagnosed, and he had lapsed once or twice and forgotten to take his meds and slipped into a psychosis – but they were firm that he had not missed any doses for a couple of years at least now, and they added that he had been gainfully employed by his step-father, with no issues arising.

Madruga and Sterling did not make it to the trailer, investigators believed. Their bodies were found the next day, just over four miles short of the trailer, but still 11 miles from the car they had abandoned. Their bodies were found on separate sides of the road. Then Huett's skeleton was found a little closer to the trailer, on the same road. A quarter of a mile north-west of the trailer, three forestry service blankets and an old flashlight were found. Mathias' body was never found.

Adding to the mystery is that on the night of their disappearance there is also a strange tale involving a man who had a heart attack, and a woman carrying a baby in the middle of the snowy wilderness, along with an eerie sound of whistling. Mr. Joseph Shones, aged fifty-five at the time, came forward to speak to the police and explain what had happened to him that night, and what he had seen. He said that he had been driving his vehicle up the same astonishingly rocky road. He said he had been checking the snow line there. The reason he was doing this, he said, was to ensure that he could fetch his wife and daughter up that weekend to go to their cabin. His car also got stuck just before the snow line; in fact, only about 50 metres from where the boys' car would later be found. He said he got out of his car and tried to push it free from the snow and frozen mud, but as he was doing so, he had a heart attack.

This was later confirmed to law enforcement by hospital doctors. Fortunately for Shones, it was only a minor heart attack and he did survive. He said that on feeling the heart attack happening, he managed to get back inside his vehicle and turn the engine on to keep warm. He said he lay back in his car and hoped for the symptoms to pass. At some time later that night he said he heard "whistling."

The whistling seemed to be coming from a little way down the road and it made him get out of his car to see who was coming. He said he saw what looked like a group of men and a woman carrying a baby. He said he could see the figures from the light glaring from another vehicle's headlights. He said he thought he could hear them talking, although they were too far off for him to hear what they said. He said he shouted out for help, but that as soon as he had done this, the headlights of the other vehicle went out, and the group talking stopped.

Confused and a little perturbed, he said he got back in his car and lay back again. Sometime later, he estimates perhaps two hours later, he claimed he saw lights close-up outside his car window. It was flashlight beams, he said. Again, he called out for help. Again, the flashlights went out and whoever was out there simply disappeared; or certainly, he could neither see nor hear them anymore.

He said he remained in his car until it ran out of gas. The engine had been on to provide warmth in the car, and then, though still dark, he began to make his way on foot back to a lodge called the Mountain House, approximately eight miles back the way he had come. On his way up the mountain drive, he had called in at the lodge to have a drink. As he began his journey back on foot, he said he passed the abandoned car of the four boys. He said that it was around this spot that he believed the voices had been coming from.

A few weeks later however, on March 10th, it was reported that the man was no longer sure what he had seen. "I was half-conscious, not lucid, hallucinating, and in a lot of pain. Whether I half-saw or half-imagined a second vehicle, I just don't know." He said that the morning after, when his wife drove him to hospital after getting home with a ride from the hostel owner, he told his wife he had seen the boys' car, but whether he'd actually seen another car too, he said he now no longer knew.

He had initially said he saw two sets of headlights on the night he had the heart attack and shouted at them for help, and he said that although he'd told his wife he'd seen a pickup truck behind the boys' car; he now did not know why he had said that and couldn't remember if he really had!

A different witness later told his wife that he had seen a pickup truck behind the boy's car at between 11pm and midnight on the night they vanished, although it is not stated in the reports where this sighting took place. Was it on the gravel forestry road or the highway?

After investigators were summoned to the abandoned park ranger's trailer in which the body of Weiher had been discovered wrapped in the shroud, a subsequent search of the vicinity discovered the body of Madruga, approximately ten miles from the trailer lying partly eaten by animals and dragged about 10 feet from the forestry road, by a stream. He was found face-up. Sterling was found in a wooded area close-by. There was nothing left of him but his bones, scattered all around.

The day after this, 40 searchers led by Sheriff Dick Stenberg found the remains of another of the missing men. Tragically, Huett's father joined the search that day, and it was he who came across the horrifying sight of what later turned out to be his son's backbone. This was North-East of the Trailer, as were the remains of Sterling and Madruga, going away from the direction of their car, at a distance of 19 miles from it. Huett's Levi jeans were there too, and his shoes. The following day, a deputy sheriff found his skull, downhill.

The Tennessean Newspaper of June the 14, 1978 wrote, 'The discovery of the bodies has revived the unanswered questions. Why DID they go up there? "It bugs the hell out of me," said Forcino, head of the Plumas County search team that looked for the men. "Every relative contacted from the five families said it was wholly out of character for the men to go off on their up the mountain." He surmises that Huett, confused and horrified after Weiher died, left to get away from the body.'

As for the families, "We know there's more to it than what's been said," Madruga's mother commented. 'With the melting of the mountain snow, some of the mystery has cleared. It is known their suffering defied description as they fought to live, at times illogically even for men of their mental impairments,' said the Tennessean. 'They drove east rather than south toward home past Lake Oroville and wound up on a mountain road until the pavement ended. They got out, it appears, and walked and ran uphill in the middle of the night into the deepening drifts!'

Could Mathias have had anything to do with his friends' deaths? He was the only one still missing. Had he slipped into a psychotic state? All the others were dead, and he was no-where to be seen. But would they not have had defensive wounds on their bodies? Would the boy wrapped in a shroud not have tried to fight back? Or had he been too scared, for weeks, as he was held there by Mathias? But how they got through 19 miles of waist-high snow still defies explanation.

Although Mathias had in the past, before medication,

occasionally been prone to aggression, he had never acted with aggression toward his four friends. Could he have maintained an aggression towards them, for weeks and weeks, cooped up inside the trailer?

The police believed Mathias too had likely died along with the rest of his friends and his body had been covered by vegetation and been buried there. But they could not find his body, even with cadaver dogs. If he had survived and it had been a case of Mathias becoming violent, it still didn't answer the question as to why he would drive miles and miles out of the way and end up on a forest road, unless he planned to kill them all – but, they died of starvation and hypothermia, not from being attacked, as far as investigators could tell.

And, how could he have made it out of there alive himself, in the waist-deep snow and pitch dark for miles on foot? He'd left his car behind. Certainly, all through their long investigation, the authorities never once suggested this tragedy was as a result of an act of violence carried out by Mathias.

'Wearing low cut shoes, they made their way an incredible 19 miles through 6-foot deep snow. A storm howled most of the night. Battle for survival in the Sierras lead to the trailer. A lone shelter in a vast wilderness. A one in a thousand chance of finding that. It took at least a day and the night to travel that distance before Weiher and possibly two others stumbled onto a snowbound Forest Service trailer. When five slightly retarded young men vanished 110 days ago, at first it looked like a terrible accident, perhaps growing out of nothing more than simple confusion over the way home. But now, with four of their bodies leaving tell-tale signs of a desperate fight for survival in the high Sierras, authorities and families aren't so sure,' said The Tennessean.

What caused these young men to drive to this very isolated, freezing, and unknown location? What caused them to abandon their still-working car? What made them walk or run for miles in 6-foot deep snow-covered pitch-dark rocky rugged land? Why didn't they walk down the road they had come up? Why were they all found in different spots? How did they manage to find an abandoned trailer, in the dark? Why wasn't all the food and the fuel in the cabin used? Why did the boy in the trailer never attempt to leave it?

"They wouldn't have fled off in the wood like a bunch of quail. We know good and well that somebody made them do it. We can't visualize someone getting the upper hand on those five men, but we know it must have been," Jack Madruga's mother said.

If someone chased them, why was the car undamaged and found as though they had been driving with pristine precision? Who had been using flashlights? And whose were the voices Mr. Shones heard on the same road? What were the whistling noises? Why would a woman be out in the snow and dark, carrying a baby?

"I can't understand why Gary would have been that scared," said Klops. "All those paperbacks and they didn't even build a lousy fire. I can't understand why they didn't do that unless they were afraid." But he cannot imagine what they were afraid of. Neither can the investigators. They can't prove there was foul play and they can't explain it if there wasn't.

If we were to make the mistake of thinking that these 'boys' were so 'mentally disabled' that's the reason they ran off into the night to certain death, well that would be an error. Two of the 'boys' had served in the US Army,

Madruga had actually not been diagnosed as being 'mentally impaired,' and Mathias, while diagnosed with schizophrenia, was managing his condition and holding down a job. Both Madruga and Mathias had been able to get driver's licenses. The label of 'mentally disabled' cannot really be used as the answer; for as a group, they weren't too mentally disabled to hold down jobs, serve in the Army, and drive.

Their car was also not irretrievably stuck. There were five of them, and they were burly enough to have shifted it. The engine worked fine, the car had gas, and they had not crashed. Why did they leave the car rather than drive away? What happened to them, or what did they see, that caused them to run from their car, abandoning all safety that night?

The driver's door was wound down. Why would that be? It was very cold. Had they been talking to someone outside the car? Or had they wound the window down to take a better look at something outside the car?

Had the 'woman with a baby' played a trick on the boys, conning them into believing she needed urgent help? Had they abandoned their car to go to her mercy? Or, had the man experiencing the heart attack simply hallucinated this woman, and the strange whistling? The five men all sounded trusting of others, according to family statements, and they were friendly boys, to the point that one of them is described as getting upset if he waved 'hello' to a stranger and the stranger didn't wave back. Did someone use the oldest trick in the book to lure them away by showing them a damsel in distress? Was it even a man with long hair?

But if so, what did she, or a group of people allegedly seen with her, want with these men? And what did they do to them? Why would they even be there, in that isolated and dark and remote place? What were they, if they existed, doing out there? There was no shelter there. The trailer the boys made it to was many miles through 6 feet of snow – which is the most mysterious aspect in all of this – just how did they wade for 20 miles in 6 feet deep snow, in light-weight clothes and shoes? – and what on earth could have made them do that?

The remains of most of the men were too decomposed to even be able to know if serious assault had taken place, although presumably their bones were tested for knife wounds and such. Presumably no such wounds were found – because the police insisted, they could find no signs of foul play.

Local people said that it is simply not possible to take a wrong turn and find yourself in the middle of the mountains and forest, and not know you are heading that way. They ended up way in the mountains in the Plumas National Forest, at an elevation impossible not to notice. It was hundreds of feet up. The main road they had been on was a dead straight road through the valley. Were they carjacked? Abducted? Did they pick up a deranged hitcher? There were five of them; but maybe a man with a gun? But what could he have wanted with them? And, in the dark when they left their car, wasn't there a good chance of rushing the man – knocking him over, fighting back? Two of them had served in the Army, and while that did not necessarily mean they had been trained in self-defence or how to fist-fight, but there were five of them.

Unless; had one of them been killed perhaps – maybe Madruga, who has never been found? Of them all, he was no doubt the most volatile, and although dosed up on his medication, would he have simply acquiesced to an abductor? Wouldn't he have resisted? Had he been killed by a crazed psychopathic hitcher and the four remaining men been so terrified that they became mute and absolutely pliable? Was this how they were managed so easily? But what kind of psychopath would keep them hostage in a trailer in the middle of nowhere, snowbound, for weeks and weeks, and wade them through 20 miles of snow to get there? Or had the boys fled in utter panic while their friend was killed?

None of it makes any sense. Had a carjacker told them to get out of the car and run while he stole the car? If so, why would he then leave the car behind? And where had this car-jacker gone? Madruga's parents said their son was obsessed with this car – it was his pride and joy and he would have been hard pressed to leave it, no matter the threat.

Melba Madruga insisted that her son would not have driven up that isolated road at night, and he would not have abandoned his car. "I'm sure he would have come home directly from the game," she said. "There is no way he would have gone voluntarily into the mountains at night," she told the Los Angeles Times.

How did they even manage to get to where they were found? Had they walked calmly off into the woods, with the plan of gaining higher ground and elevation because they believed the car was irreversibly stuck? But why not go the easy route, back down the road where the snow was not up to 10 feet deep? Search and Rescue teams will sometimes point out that common sense is lost once a person gets lost, and that it's often easier in a person's mind to go forward and to higher ground rather than re-trace their steps; after all, they know what is behind them, and if it was miles and miles of road but no houses, no shelter and no help, maybe the boys thought it best to progress upward and forward to seek aid and shelter. But the boys knew the snow was not waist-high back down the road. Surely the path of least resistance would have made them turn around and walk back along the road? Or, just stay in the car for the night in the hope that someone might come along and rescue them. But did something scare them so badly that they fled the safety of the car and fled into the woods? If so, what could that have been? It was as though they had fled for their lives.

Did one of them panic in the dark and cold and jump out of the car because they thought the car was stuck in the snow and then fled in a sudden onset of hysteria? – resulting in the others also panicking and fleeing too? It's possible, but it doesn't make any sense, and what still doesn't seem possible is that he, whichever one he was, would have then been followed by the other four into the snow-filled wilderness. You would think one if not all of them would have stopped pretty quickly after becoming immersed in the snow.

Why were they too scared to leave the trailer? Why did they not eat all of the dried food rations – they had found some of the food and eaten it, why not the rest? And, why not turn on the heat? Were they so scared of something outside that they kept as silent and still as possible inside the trailer? If no-one was with the boys, it can only surely be surmised that they were in mortal fear of their lives from something that was outside the trailer. But what?

I hope you have enjoyed this book. If you have enjoyed it, perhaps you would be kind enough to leave a **Review**,

Thank you so much, Steph

Some of these tales can also be heard on my podcast on iTunes: Tales of Mystery Unexplained

https://podcasts.apple.com/us/podcast/tales-of-mystery-unexplained/id1216208205

https://www.patreon.com/stephyoungpodcast

Other Books by Steph Young: https://www.amazon.com/Steph-Young/e/B00KE8B6B0/

**Twisted Tales of Mystery Unexplained**

**Creepy Tales of Mystery Unexplained**

**Something in The Woods is Taking People**

**You can't escape The Woods**

**Tales for After-Dark: True Ghost Stories**

**People Missing in the Woods: True Stories of Unexplained Disappearances**

**True Stories of Monstrous Creatures**

**Desolating Spirits** and many more.....

**Please go to StephYoungAuthor.com if you would like to stay up to date with new releases.**

**You can also find me here:**

**Facebook**

**Instagram**

**Twitter**

I hope you have enjoyed this book. If you have enjoyed it, perhaps you would be kind enough to leave a **Review**,

Thank you so much, Steph

Printed in Great Britain
by Amazon